An old print of South Place Chapel in Finsbury, very much as it was when the first Concert was given in 1887. A handbill advertising this Concert is shown on page 16.

A HUNDRED YEARS of CHAMBER MUSIC

by

Frank V. Hawkins

SOUTH PLACE ETHICAL SOCIETY

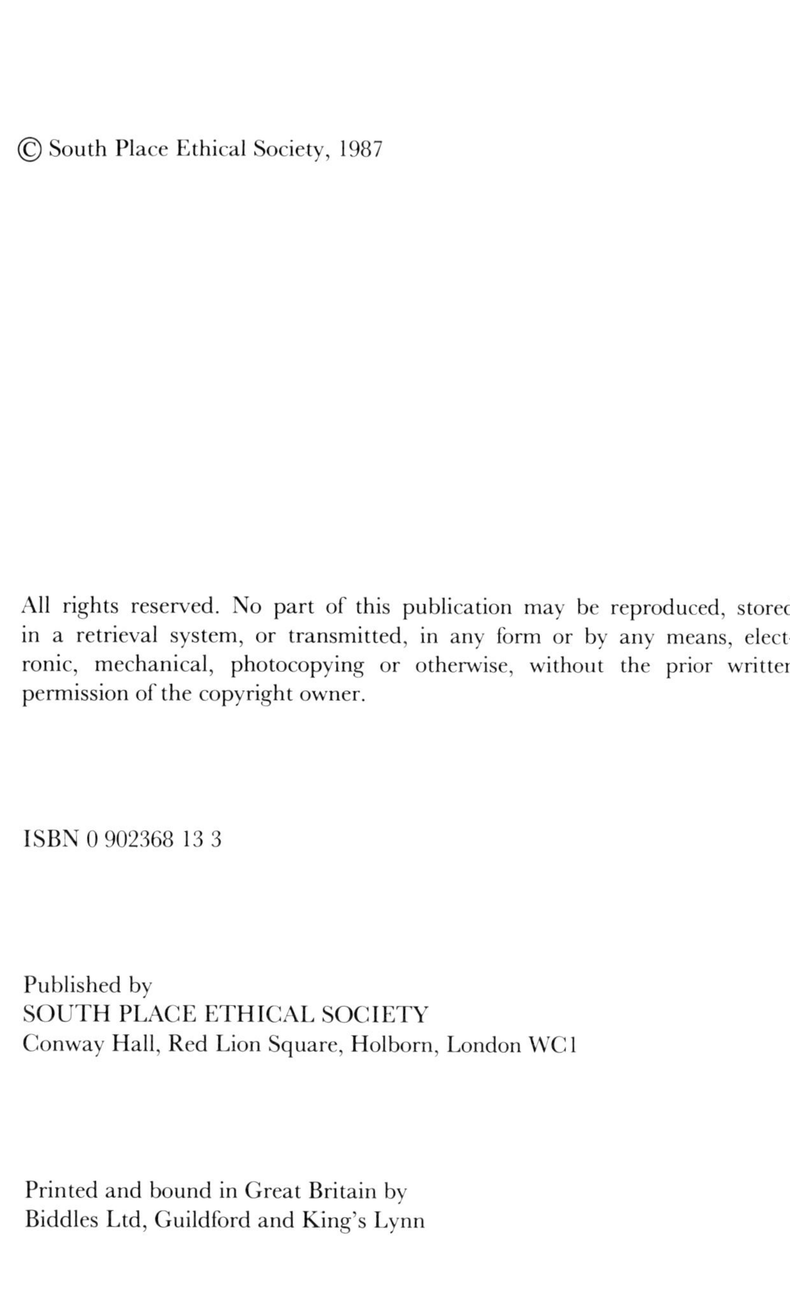

ISBN 0 902368 13 3

Published by
SOUTH PLACE ETHICAL SOCIETY
Conway Hall, Red Lion Square, Holborn, London WC1

Printed and bound in Great Britain by
Biddles Ltd, Guildford and King's Lynn

CONTENTS

ILLUSTRATIONS

Illustrations (contd.) Page

FOREWORD

Harry Blech, C.B.E.

It is not quite 100 years since my father took me to listen to Beethoven String Quartets at the old South Place in Finsbury. I must have been about eleven or twelve at the time and had been playing the violin for only two or three years. Sleep overtook me quickly I remember and I do not know whether it was early or late Beethoven. Since then things have improved and any Beethoven Quartet well played will now keep me wide awake at any time of the day or night.

That the South Place Concerts have played an important part in the remarkable growth of the public appreciation of chamber music in London is self-evident; but just as important has been the permanent platform the concerts have supplied for aspiring and promising musicians.

In 1891 in a London newspaper called "The World" the following appeared: "I take the opportunity, however, of mentioning the admirable way in which things are kept going at South Place . . . The programmes are in no way less severe than those at St. James's Hall; . . . If one of our prosperous West-enders would go down some Sunday and put into the plate the same percentage of his week's income as that contributed by his Finsbury neighbour, he would make the committee's mind easy for the rest of the season."

The writer of this article was none other than George Bernard Shaw who at the time was making his living as music critic of the above mentioned newspaper. What would he have said at this Centenary of their concerts which only the bombing of London in the last war interrupted? For in spite of this long passage of time and the growing enthusiasm of the musical public for chamber music the South Place is still the only Society which provides a weekly concert of this kind for the general public. A most remarkable achievement.

Radio and recordings have of course brought outstanding performances to us, but the great international ensembles (and I include in this category many of our own quartets) still appear sporadically in public, albeit more often than the annual visits in my youth of the Busch or Lener quartets.

The book the Society published to celebrate its 2,000th concert in 1969 is in itself a remarkable document. In it you will find not only a record of all the compositions that have survived the passage of time and fashion but of those thousands of musicians that have aspired to spending their lives in exploring the spiritual wonders of the great masterpieces of chamber music.

I did not think in 1950, when I took part at Conway Hall in the last concert of the Blech String Quartet, that I would have the honour thirty-six years later of writing a foreword to their Centenary Book. May they find the strength and fortitude to continue for the next century and perhaps build their own concert hall.

Harry Blech

ACKNOWLEDGEMENTS

This book is an up-dating (by the same author) of "The Story of Two Thousand Concerts" and up to the point of the 2000th Concert the main text is reprinted with a few emendations. The first half of that book was in any case based on W.S. Meadmore's "The Story of a Thousand Concerts".

What virtue the concerts may have comes from the loyal support and ungrudging service of the artists. In this book, inevitably, there are serious omissions of acknowledgment. But the Lists which we have done our best to make correct and complete, show the extent and value of that support which we acknowledge with gratitude.

Much of the interest of this book lies in the articles provided by many of the ensembles who have played at our Concerts. We thank these busy professional musicians for sparing the time to provide them for us. Mr. Leslie Orrey's article on the London Scene in 1887 is a fascinating contribution. The rest of the book represents a tremendous team effort by the Concert Committee which prepared the publication in 1969 of "The Story of Two Thousand Concerts." It involved much research back to 1887, much laborious preparation of statistics and the continuous checking, re-checking and correcting of facts and figures by busy people with many other commitments, devoting their already meagre leisure to a monumental, albeit worthwhile task.

Special Sub-Committee for "The Story of Two Thousand Concerts" Eileen Barralet, Joan Hutchinson, *Mary Lincé, Colin Barralet, Charles Browne, Peter Costello, *Frank Hawkins, *George Hutchinson, *Martin Lincé.

---

*Also responsible for the preparation of "A Hundred Years of Chamber Music".

ALFRED J. CLEMENTS
Organiser and Hon. Secretary
1887-1938

A series of chamber music extending over one hundred years including over 2400 concerts must surely be unique. This achievement was only made possible in the first place by the idealism and indefatigable efforts of A. J. Clements and the endeavours of his successors inspired by his example. Mr. Clements was Secretary and Organiser from 1887 up to his death in 1938. From the time that the idea was first mooted that these concerts should be managed by a South Place Committee, Mr. Clements displayed a genius for arranging programmes and getting the best possible artists to perform them. More remarkable was the brilliant foresight which enabled him to visualise an audience which would come Sunday after Sunday and listen to programmes which rarely if ever were to make any concession to popular taste, but contained only the very finest inspirations of chamber music composers! Even in the early days of the concerts he was a practical visionary. The history of the concerts is indeed a glowing testimony to unusual gifts revealed in the building up of programmes, and the inclusion of new works, no mean achievement in itself, as all who have tried to promote concerts will appreciate. Frequenters of the Concerts well know the number of such works that have been performed and it is Clements and the maintenance of his tradition that has made this possible.

In 1927 Mr. Clements was awarded the Cobbett Gold Medal for his services to Chamber Music.

The Second World War was a watershed in the history of the Concerts. They had to close down when most of the players were called up, as indeed were many of the Concert Committee. Mrs. Clements, now in her eighties, carried on for two seasons after the war, assisted by Florence Hawkins. In 1947 George Hutchinson became Hon. Secretary. He had served under Alfred Clements as Assistant Secretary since 1931 and this apprenticeship had been invaluable. However, conditions after the Second World War were different. Free admission had to be abandoned and a small ticket price introduced - one shilling (i.e. 5 new pence). The Arts Council subsidised an increase in the flat rate payment to artists and later the GLC and the London Borough of Camden helped out. The composition of the programmes also changed - long programmes based on an ensemble plus solo piano plus singer were no longer possible or acceptable; they were replaced by a String Quartet with an occasional Song Cycle Recital and hardly ever a Piano Recital. In the early days ensembles were very often ad hoc, got together for an occasion. There were about five established Quartets. Now there are over twenty high quality English teams, many of international status.

GEORGE HUTCHINSON
Hon. Secretary
1947-1986

In 1985 George Hutchinson was made an MBE for his services to music.

FRANK ANDRADE HAWKINS
Honorary Treasurer 1905-1929

ALBERT MARTIN LINCÉ
Honorary Treasurer 1951-1987

A HUNDRED YEARS AGO
The London Scene, 1887

The following is taken from an article in "The Story of 2000 Concerts" (1969) written by the late Leslie Orrey who had been Head of Goldsmiths' College.

"Sabbatarians may shudder but a series of Sunday concerts is in course at the South Place Institute, Finsbury." So runs the first mention in a London musical periodical of the South Place Concerts, intended by their promoters "to provide aesthetic and intellectual entertainments on the dull English Sunday."

Sundays may have been dull, but Londoners were not at other times starved of music in that Jubilee year. On Good Friday, 1887, "within four miles of Charing Cross" could be heard not only several *Stabat Maters* (Rossini, of course) but at least twelve *Messiahs*, one at the Albert Hall drawing some 7,000. At St. James's Hall that day there were no fewer than three concerts, while "the Japanese Village was crammed". The Japanese Village was in Hyde Park, on the site of the 1851 Exhibition; but for its presence there *The Mikado* might never have been written.

Londoners had no need to travel to Sydenham for their orchestral fare. There was the Royal Philharmonic Society, revered and venerable; Richter and Henschel were Mann's rivals at St. James's Hall. The thirst for choral music could be assuaged by the Sacred Harmonic Society, the Novello Oratorio Concerts, Mr. Leslie's Choir, the Bach Choir. Kensington, Kennington, Brixton were alive with choral societies; while Walthamstow, quite in the modern manner, could boast a three-day "Festival" on its own, "established by an amateur, Mr. J.H.H. Read, in a new and spacious hall built at Mr. Read's expense". A yet more ambitious scheme was taking shape in Mile End, where on 14th May Her Majesty the Queen opened the new and resplendent People's Palace.

Victorian London had in fact a rich musical life, but never on Sundays - never, that is, until the South Place Concerts.

Yet another extract from Meadmore's book was reprinted in "The Story of Two Thousand Concerts" and is again reprinted here in full:

ORIGIN OF THE CONCERTS

It was in 1878 that the People's Concert Society was formed for the purpose of "increasing the popularity of good music by means of cheap concerts". Various centres in the less opulent parts of London were selected as being suitable venues, and as a result of negotiations initiated by Conrad Thies, a member of the South Place Society, concerts were given at South Place. It is interesting to recall that in these early days no audience was expected to listen to the four movements of a quartet without some light respite. In 1887 the PCS had to cut their season short for lack of funds. Thereupon A.J. Clements, J.H.K. Todd, and some other members of South Place formed a Committee and gave seven concerts. The PCS then asked this Committee if they would continue their work, but were told that although they might not be young in years they were in concert-giving, and that the experience of seven concerts was hardly sufficient to justify the undertaking of a six months' season. The Committee, however, suggested that if the PCS would arrange the programmes for the first three months, they would undertake the remainder of the season. This was agreed to, and from that time the South Place Concert Committee took over the whole of the work, and the PCS were set free to open a new centre in another part of London, which they promptly did.

The concerts were called the South Place Sunday Popular Concerts, but why the word "Popular" was introduced into the title must have been a cause of bewilderment to many. Indeed, a member of the Committee recalls overhearing the following conversation: "Is this a classical concert?" "I don't know, it's a Brahms concert". "Oh, I suppose they never do 'The Country

Girl'?" The title was, in fact, a misnomer, for the music has always been of the most consistently *un*popular character. It must also be remembered that when the concerts were first commenced public taste was all for the lighter forms of music, and that actually South Place did a vast amount of spade work in creating an appreciative audience for chamber music.

SOUTH PLACE INSTITUTE,

SOUTH PLACE, FINSBURY.

(Close to BROAD STREET and MOORGATE STREET STATIONS).

A

SERIES

OF

Vocal & Instrumental

CONCERTS

WILL BE GIVEN AT

THE ABOVE INSTITUTE

On SUNDAY EVENINGS, COMMENCING FEBRUARY 20th,

And continuing on successive Sundays until further notice. 1887

To commence at 7 o'clock. Doors open at 6.30.

ADMISSION FREE. Collection to defray expenses.

The following Artists will appear at the first Concert, Sunday, Feb. 20th :—

Herr HENKEL (Violin).

Herr SCHRATTENHOLZ (Violin).

Mr. W. A. EASTON (Viola).

Signor PERUZZI (Violoncello).

Vocalist: Mr. HERBERT THORNDIKE.

FOR FURTHER PARTICULARS SEE PROGRAMMES.

Communications, or Contributions in aid of the Concert Expenses, may be sent to the Hon. Sec., ALFRED J. CLEMENTS ; or the Hon. Treasurer, JOHN H. K. TODD, at the Institute.

SOUTH PLACE INSTITUTE,

SOUTH PLACE, FINSBURY, E.C.

SUNDAY EVENING VOCAL AND INSTRUMENTAL CONCERTS.

First Concert of the Series,

SUNDAY, FEBRUARY 20, 1887.

1st Violin ... ... HERR HENKEL.
2nd Violin ... ... HERR SCHRATTENHOLZ.
Viola ... ... MR. W. A. EASTON.
Violoncello ... ... SIGNOR PERUZZI.
Vocalist ... ... MR. HERBERT THORNDIKE.
Accompanist .. ... MR. CHARLES IMHOF.

PROGRAMME AND WORDS OF THE SONGS

1. QUARTET IN D MINOR .... *Mozart.* (*b.* 1756, *d.* 1791.)

(For Two Violins, Viola, and Violoncello.)

Allegro moderato.
Andante.
Menuetto and Trio: Allegretto.
Allegretto ma non troppo.

2. SONG.... "Thou'rt passing hence" .... *Sullivan.* (*b.* 1842.)

MR. HERBERT THORNDIKE.

Thou'rt passing hence, my brother,
Oh, my earliest friend, farewell!
Thou'rt leaving me without thy voice
In a lonely home to dwell;
And from the hills, and from the hearth,
And from the household tree,
With thee departs the lingering mirth
The brightness goes with thee.

But thou, my friend, my brother,
Thou'rt speeding to the shore,
Where the dirge-like tones of parting words
Shall smite thy soul no more;
And thou wilt see our holy dead,
The lost on earth and main,
Into the sheaf of kindred hearts
Thou wilt be bound again.

Then tell our white-haired father,
That in the paths he trod,
The child he loved, the last on earth,
Yet walks and worships God;
Say that his last fond blessing, yet
Rests on my heart like dew,
And by its hallowing might I trust
Once more his face to view.

And tell our gentle mother,
That on her grave I pour
The sorrows of my spirit forth,
As on her breast of yore;
Happy thou art that soon—how soon,
Our good and bright will see,
Oh! brother, brother, may I dwell
Ere long with them and thee!

3. VIOLONCELLO SOLO—

"Adagio from the 3rd Concerto".. *Goltermann.* (*d.* 1876.)

Signor PERUZZI.

4. SONG. ...."Sunday"............ *Brahms.* (*b.* 1833.)

MR. HERBERT THORNDIKE.

Six weary days are passed and over,
Since I my true love gazed on last,
And that was upon a Sunday,
By her dwelling as I pass'd.
She stood before the cottage door,
A thousand pretty looks she wore.
Would to heaven I were with her this day!

Six pleasant days are past and over
Since a look on me she cast,
And that was upon a Sunday,
In the church door as she pass'd;
That look of her I'll ne'er forget,
A thousand times I think of it.
Would to heaven I were with her this day!

Page 1 of programme

HELEN HENSCHEL

GERVASE ELWES

PLUNKET GREENE

JOHN SAUNDERS

A HUNDRED YEARS OF CHAMBER MUSIC

by FRANK V. HAWKINS*

1887-1897

February 20th, 1887 was the date of the first Concert and it opened with Mozart's D minor string quartet K.421. Herbert Thorndike, an uncle of Dame Sybil, sang and was accompanied by Charles Imhof, a member of the family of the West End musical firm.

During the first season seven concerts were given, during the second season thirteen and as early as the third season, that is 1888/89, weekly concerts throughout the winter were given. This practice has continued ever since with the exception of the second world war. During this third season several well-known musicians appeared for the first time at the Concerts, one of these being the Irish singer Harry Plunket Greene, who started a long and valuable association which lasted until his death in 1936. His last appearance was in 1935. It is perhaps true to say that he continued to sing at an age when others might have retired but there exists a recording made towards the end of his

---

*Frank V. Hawkins was born in 1929. Earlier in that year his father, Frank A. Hawkins, died. He had been on the South Place Concert Committee and its Treasurer since 1905. His mother worked on the Concert Committee from 1922, becoming an Assistant Secretary in 1947, which post she held up to her death in 1967. Frank (jun.) became a member of the Concert Committee in 1945 and Assistant Secretary in 1967.

He studied viola and horn at the Royal College of Music and was professional horn player in England until 1976, when he started to work abroad. Since 1979 he has had a position in an orchestra in West Germany where he is able to play both his instruments, and his connection with the Concerts remains unbroken as he returns to England every year for the months of November, December and January. He regards himself as a horn player who enjoys playing string quartets.

life of Schubert's "Der Leiermann". He put his age to poignant use in this sad song about the old hurdy-gurdy man standing barefoot on the ice and nobody throwing him any coins.

In the same season the Walenn family appeared as a string quartet. Herbert Walenn was for many years a professor at the Royal Academy of Music and head of the London Violoncello School. Another famous musician appearing in this season was Adolf Borsdorf, horn player and father of three horn playing sons who later also appeared at the Concerts. He taught at the Royal College of Music until 1923 and nearly every present-day professional player of the horn is either his pupil, his pupil's pupil or his pupil's pupil's pupil. He was a founder member of the London Symphony Orchestra and its first chairman.

In the fourth season, 1890/91, viola player Alfred Hobday, another founder member of the London Symphony Orchestra, started a family association with these concerts which lasted for fifty years. His appearance in this season was followed by the first appearance in the 1899/1900 season of his double-bass playing brother Claude and his wife, pianist Ethel Hobday, played in 1913. Also in this season Hans Wessely played. He led a string quartet with Spencer Dyke (1899/1900)* as second violin, Ernest Tomlinson (1901/02) viola (no relation to the light music composer of the same name) and B. Patterson Parker, cello (1893/94). After the first world war Spencer Dyke became leader and Edwin Quaife joined as second violin. With Ernest Tomlinson, viola, and B. Patterson Parker, cello, the quartet continued until the latter's death in 1930.

There is a recording of the Brahms clarinet quintet made by Frederick Thurston (1923/24) and the Spencer Dyke quartet. Thurston, known affectionately as "Jack" by the profession, made many appearances both at South Place and at Conway Hall. He played the Brahms quintet on October 10th, 1951 and his last appearance at the Concerts (in Brahms' trio for clarinet, cello and piano) was on October 12th, 1952, his association with the Concerts having lasted thirty years. He died, too soon, in December, 1953.

---

*Throughout the rest of this article dates expressed in this way signify the season in which the artist mentioned played for the Concerts for the first time.

Another devoted friend of the Concerts who died prematurely was violinist John Saunders (1891) who played at no fewer than 239 Concerts over the next 27 years. His fellow musicians admired him so much that they clubbed together and bought him a Stradivarius. The Strad was presented in 1916 but John Saunders lived only three years to enjoy it. When he died, in October, 1919, it was learned that not only had he refused more lucrative engagements in order to play at South Place but also on several occasions paid for the cost of extra instrumentalists. A scholarship in his memory was founded at the Guildhall School of Music and the proceeds of five South Place Concerts amounting to £308 were given to the fund. His portrait hangs in the library at Conway Hall.

During the 1893/94 season A.E. Brain (senior) played the horn. Six members of the family (four of them horn players) have played for us; his sons Alfred and Aubrey (horns) at the old South Place Institute and at Conway Hall Aubrey's widow, Muriel (viola), his sons Leonard (oboe and cor anglais) and Dennis, perhaps the most outstanding horn player of our time, who was so tragically killed in a car accident in 1957.

The year 1894 was the year in which Richard H. Walthew wrote offering his services in the following letter:

> "Dear Sir
>
> Having attended many of the admirable concerts given every Sunday at South Place I am writing to offer my services as pianist.
>
> I am very sensible of the great good that these concerts are doing in making known the masterpieces of music to a public fed mostly on comic songs and shop ballads, and I should like to associate myself with the work.
>
> I am Dear Sir
>
> Your obedient servant,
>
> Richard H. Walthew A.R.C.M."

This distinguished musician - pianist, conductor and composer - maintained his association with us until 1951, appearing at 217 concerts. Some of the Concerts were entirely devoted to his compositions. His last appearance as a performer was in 1940 but he remained on the panel of adjudicators of the Clements Memorial Prize (mentioned later in this book) until his death.

The next season 1895/96 saw the first appearance of violinist Jessie Grimson. She was a member of a family who formed a complete string octet which performed more than once at the Concerts. She herself played many times, usually leading her own string quartet.

Charles Draper, clarinet, played during the tenth season 1897/98 and lovers of old recordings will recall the famous record he made with the Lener String Quartet of Mozart's clarinet quintet. Also during this season Samuel Liddle, who was the "Gerald Moore" of an earlier generation, commenced an association which lasted until 1940. We remember him particularly as Plunket Greene's accompanist. Gerald Moore himself played for the first time in the 1928/29 season.

1898-1907

The 1898/99 season saw the first appearance of the fine viola player Lionel Tertis, who brought to public notice the full qualities of his chosen instrument, and the cellist, Charles Crabbe, another London Symphony Orchestra founder member. Both these men lived to a very great age: Crabbe died in 1965 and Tertis in 1975, not quite a hundred years old. By 1927 Charles Crabbe had appeared 97 times at the Concerts, mainly in quartets led either by John Saunders or Charles Woodhouse. Charles Woodhouse (1900-01) appeared more than 190 times. He was leader of the Queen's Hall Orchestra and the old Royal Philharmonic Orchestra and his name lives on as an editor of orchestral parts. He had a brother, Frederick Woodhouse (1921-22) who sang many times for us.

We quote here a letter from Sir Hamilton Harty who first appeared as a pianist in 1900/01. "Very many thanks for the charming calendar, and the parts of the 4tet. My Symphony has had the good fortune to win the prize and I think it shd sound fairly well as it is much the best thing I have done yet! - H. Harty."

In 1901/02 May Mukle, another member of a famous musical family, made her first appearance, her last being in 1946. In 1902/02 two well-known names appeared in their now almost forgotten rôles as pianist and violinist respectively: the conductor Sir (then Mr.) Henry J. Wood and the composer Frank Bridge.

The following letter was sent by pianist Evelyn Suart (1903/04) to my father (as treasurer) - it illustrates the generous attitude of many artists to the Concerts: "Dear Mr. Hawkins, Thank you so much for sending my fee, which I am always glad to receive, so as to have the great pleasure of paying it back into the South Place Concert funds. I also enclose a penny stamp, so that the funds do not even lose that amount at my hand. It is always enjoyable to me to work for South Place, where such ideal conditions are reached . . ."

In the same season Frederic Austin appeared as a singer; it was he who arranged the "Beggar's Opera" in the famous production which ran for three and a half years at Hammersmith after the first world war. Josef Holbrooke performed as a pianist. His views on the neglect of his compositions are expressed on the following postcard: "I did not get your 1914 report, but I saw one at Saunders. I hope you will not ignore my work again this year as you do. One tries to get assistance for good fiddles for fiddlers but the poor composer is heard *once or twice a year.* Do you think it just? Yours ever, Holbrooke. P.S. Not *too* much *German* music!"

Holbrooke's trio for piano, horn and violin was heard at a South Place Concert as recently as the 31st October, 1965.

Gervase Elwes, another great friend of South Place, sang for the first time in the 1903/04 season. He had given the first performance of Vaughan Williams' song cycle "On Wenlock Edge" (an early recording exists) and it has always been associated with his name. His tragic early death in a railway accident in America was a profound shock to the musical profession. The Musicians' Benevolent Fund was founded in his memory. At South Place the proceeds of a Concert were devoted to the Fund and it has since become the custom to hold a Concert each year for the benefit of this charity.

Two composers, famous in very different ways, appeared in the 1904/05 season as pianists. Percy Grainger and Sir Charles Stanford, the latter having a concert devoted to his own music which included arrangements of old Irish melodies sung by Plunket Greene. The much loved cellist, Ivor James, played for the first time during this season. His influence as a trainer for chamber music players extended to nearly every British ensemble heard at South Place Concerts and elsewhere. He last appeared as speaker at the Musicians' Benevolent Fund Concert in 1959.

Another very famous Irish singer, the tenor John McCormack, made a single appearance in 1907.

1909-1921

Two violinists appeared for the first time in the 1909/10 season - Albert Sammons (leading the New Quartet, later known as the London String Quartet) and Marjorie Hayward who later often played at the Concerts leading her own quartet. Both maintained a long association with the Concerts, Sammons until just before the second war and Marjorie Hayward until 1949/50. Ella Ivimey, a fellow student with Marjorie Hayward in Prague where they had studied under the famous violin teacher Sevčík, began her long association with the Concerts in 1917 and played as a pianist at 67 of them, although she had started her career as a violinist. She was one of the few players to become an active member of the Concert Committee on which she served from 1940 until her death in 1952. At one time she was Dame Nellie Melba's accompanist.

Isidore Schwiller first played for the Concerts on 11th December, 1910. He was a good friend who often helped Mr. Clements to get together an ensemble for unusual works, such as Schönberg's "Verklärte Nacht". In connexion with this work the Concert Committee minutes of January 1935 state "the Secretary spoke of the enthusiasm and self-sacrifice of Mr. Schwiller and his colleagues." Many of the players who cooperated with him were to become well-known performers in the chamber-music world.

In the 1911/12 season another long friendship began: Johanne Stockmarr, the Danish pianist, played for the first time. She came over every year (except during the first world war) to play at these Concerts until her death during the second world war. Two composers also appeared during this season: S. Coleridge Taylor of "Hiawatha" fame as an accompanist and Dr. (later Sir) George Henschel as a singer accompanying himself on the piano. This giant among music, a personal friend of Brahms, Tschaikovsky and Dvořák had the unique experience of founding an orchestra (the Boston Symphony Orchestra) in 1881 and returning in 1931 aged 81 to conduct at its fiftieth anniversary concert. His daughter, Helen, had a long association with the Concerts. She will be remembered by the generation which grew up with the radio "Children's Hour" for her talks about music. Her first appearance was in 1913/14, the same season as conductor-composer Eugene Goossens, who played in a string quartet as second violin!

In the 1915/16 season Benno Moisiewitsch and Daisy Kennedy appeared for the first time and played sonatas to a very large and enthusiastic audience. The Belgian violinist Ysaÿe also made a first appearance, as did André Mangeot, whose association lasted over twenty years. Another first was Harold Craxton, for many years a professor at the Royal Academy of Music. His daughter Janet (oboe) played for the Concerts for the first time in the season 1960/61.

Two singers, famous in their own right but associated with long running shows were Frederick Ranalow and Arthur Cranmer who appeared in this season. Frederick Ranalow was 'MacHeath" in the Frederic Austin "Beggar's Opera" already mentioned (which was conducted by Eugene Goossens) and Arthur Cranmer sang the "Cobbler's Song" in "Chu Chin Chow".

Two more composers appeared as accompanists: Herbert Howells in the 1918/19 season and Roger Quilter in the 1919/20 season. String players who appeared for the first time in the 1920/21 season were violinist Bessie Rawlins who continued to play for the Concerts until 1948, viola player Bernard Shore who last appeared in 1957 as a speaker at the annual Musicians' Benevolent Fund Concert and cellist Giovanni Barbirolli, now better known as conductor Sir John Barbirolli. In the same season appeared another musical knight - but not then - singer Keith Falkner, later the Director of the Royal College of Music.

1922-1933

Another singer who accompanied himself in the Henschel tradition was Michael Head (1922/23). In the same season Ethel Bartlett and Rae Robertson - two pianos - (who were to become internationally famous) commenced an association which lasted for 30 years. George Stratton, who appeared as leader of the Wood Smith Quartet, later led his own quartet of which the present Aeolian String Quartet is a direct descendant.

Yet another composer, E.J. Moeran, appeared as accompanist in 1923/24. Several artists who have had connexions with South Place for at least forty years played in the 'twenties for the first time: Marie Wilson (1923/24) remembered as co-leader of the BBC Symphony Orchestra who led her own quartet as did Antonio Brosa (1925/26); two cellists - Antony Pini (1925) (in earlier days the cellist of Brosa's quartet) and John Moore (1926). John Moore and Watson Forbes (1932/33) viola were together in the Stratton Quartet, later the Aeolian Quartet. William Primrose, the famous viola player, played the violin in the 1924/25 season.

ETHEL BARTLETT

RAE ROBERTSON

THOUSANDTH CONCERT

The Thousandth Concert was held on February 20th, 1927, exactly forty years after the first Concert. The programme, a marathon by any standard, was as follows:

1,000th CONCERT

40th Anniversary of the First Concert, Sunday, Feb. 20th, 1887.

The figures following the Artists' names denote the number of their appearances.

1. Sonata in D minor Op. 108 for Pianoforte and Violin............*Brahms*
(Eleventh time at these Concerts.)
Mrs. Ethel Hobday (23) and Mr. Albert Sammons (21).
2. Song Cycle—An Irish Idyll (in Six Miniatures) Op. 77............*Stanford*
Mr. Plunket Greene (36). At the Piano: Mr. S. Liddle (22).
3. Quartet in E flat, Op. 64, No. 6..*Haydn*
(Third time at these Concerts.)
The Spencer Dyke String Quartet: Mr. Spencer Dyke (31), Mr. Edwin Quaife (9), Mr. Ernest Tomlinson (78), Mr. B. Patterson Parker (87).
4. Songs: (*a*) Das Wandern *Schubert.* (*b*) Wiegenlied *Humperdinck.* (*c*) Ständchen *R. Strauss.*
Miss Helen Henschel (13) (to her own accompaniment).
5. Pianoforte Solo—Andante in F.......................................*Beethoven*
Mr. Richard H. Walthew (183).
6. Violin Solo—La Folia..*Corelli-Leonard*
Mr. Sidney Bowman (1). At the Piano: Mr. Sidney Harrison (1).
(First holder of the John Saunders* Scholarship.)
7. Phantasy Quintet in E minor and major.............................*Walthew*
(Dedicated to W. W. Cobbett, Esq.) (Sixth time at these Concerts.)
The Composer, Mr. Charles Woodhouse (169), Mr. Ernest Yonge (174), Mr. Charles A. Crabbe (96), Mr. Claude Hobday (13).
8. Songs—(*a*) Clear and Cool } (from Kingsley's
(*b*) I once had a sweet little doll } " Water Babies ")
(*c*) Morning Hymn
Miss Helen Henschel. ....*Henschel*
9. Pianoforte Solo—Alla Minueto, ma poco più lento..................*Grieg*
Mrs. Mildred Conway Sawyer (5).
10. Song—(*a*) Dirge in Woods
(*b*) The child and the twilight
(*c*) A lover's garland
(*d*) The Laird o' Cockpen
Mr. Plunket Greene. At the Piano: Mr. S. Liddle.
11. Octet in E flat, Op. 20...*Mendelssohn*
(Fourteenth time at these Concerts.)
Miss Jessie Grimson (105), Mr. Charles Woodhouse, Mr. Herbert Kinsey (15), Miss Jessie Stewart (15), Mr. James Lockyer (18), Mr. Ernest Yonge, Mr. B. Patterson Parker, Mr. Charles A. Crabbe.

* John Saunders (1867-1919) was for many years one of the staunchest supporters of the concerts, at which he made 239 appearances. During the season of 1919-20 five memorial concerts were held to the memory of this great artist, and, as a result of these, the Committee were able to contribute over £308 to the John Saunders Scholarship Fund.

At the end of the season, a hundred years (and a day) after Beethoven's death, a Beethoven Concert was given. It was not only the last Concert of the season but also the last to be held in the South Place Institute, an emotional occasion as the capacity audience (many had to be turned away) led by the evening's singer Christine McClure accompanied by Richard H. Walthew joined in the singing of "Auld Lang Syne" at the end of the Concert. The Institute was later demolished; the site for Conway Hall had already been purchased but two years passed before the hall was built and during these two years the Concerts were held in the City of London School at Blackfriars.

This was a difficult time for the Concerts and there was a falling off in attendance. The loss of the old familiar surroundings perhaps contributed to this. It was only during the second season at Blackfriars that it was discovered that the hall was not licensed for music so in order to conform with the law it was necessary to form "The South Place Sunday Concert Society", of which only members could be admitted. This meant enrolling members for a nominal sum. (Fortunately this break in the tradition of free admission was only to last until the end of the 1928/29 season). The temporary premises left much to be desired: on the programme of the first Concert there on October 2nd, 1927, Mr. Clements wrote the terse comment "hall not heated". He had to repeat this comment on nine of the eleven programmes from October to December, 1927. Other halls were considered but for various reasons could not be used.

Among those who made their first appearances during this period was William Busch, pianist and composer, whose premature death in 1945 was a great loss. Harry Isaacs and Solomon, pianists, and Steuart Wilson, singer, appeared for the first time in the 1927/28 season.

The 1928/29 season opened like the previous one with a Concert by the Brosa String Quartet. During this season this quartet generously gave their services at three Concerts outside the Sunday series in aid of the Conway Hall building fund. These Concerts, held on Wednesday evenings, included a piano quintet in each of which the quartet was joined by a distinguished pianist - Harriet Cohen, Mark Hambourg and Solomon. The centenary of Schubert's death fell on November 19th and on November 18th a special Schubert Concert was given including the octet, led by Isidore Schwiller who was also responsible for assembling the team. The works of Schubert also figured prominently in other Concerts during the season.

It is a remarkable testimonial to Alfred J. Clements' idealism, not to say other-worldliness, that at the foot of the programme other musical activities were advertised, including chamber music concerts given at the same time (at the Working Men's College, Crowndale Road) in direct competition with the South Place Concerts. Douglas Cameron, cello, (later in the Blech and London quartets) and Gerald Moore appeared for the first time in this season.

In June, 1929 my father died. He had been treasurer of the Concerts for 24 years and during that time had organised the appeals for buying a Stradivarius for John Saunders (presented in 1916), the John Saunders scholarship at the Guildhall School of Music (1922) and the "Clements Presentation" (1924). The first Concert of the 1929/30 season, the first in Conway Hall, began with the Andante Cantabile from Mozart's C major quartet played in my father's memory, the audience standing. The post of treasurer to the Concerts was taken by Andrew Watson who held it until the war.

The first appearance of the Griller Quartet was on December lst, 1929. They played two quartets (both in D minor though separated by songs and piano solos) Dvořák Op. 34 and Mozart K.421 - the Mozart they played on their last appearance on October 7th, 1945. On March 9th, 1930 a Concert was devoted to the works of Richard H. Walthew in which the composer appeared as pianist and his son Richard S. Walthew made his first appearance as clarinettist. The report for this season states that there were twenty-eight new instrumentalists and nine new vocalists - "this policy naturally brings in its train one of the many difficulties - that of hearing new performers without seeming to neglect well-tried friends". Eda Kersey, a violinist who died too soon, Victoria Anderson and Viola Morris who sang together as "The English Duo", Winifred Copperwheat and Norina Semino (later viola and cello of the Zorian String Quartet), Lilly and Nancy Philips, cello and violin, Alan Bush (as pianist) and singers Gwen Catley and Sophie Wyss were among the newcomers.

The Ensemble Players, led by Eda Kersey, opened the 1930/31 season which was remarkable for the performances of all the nine Dvořák string quartets which had been published up to that time. In order to fulfil this task an extra concert which included the then recently published F minor quartet was given by the Griller String Quartet at the end of the season. The list of first appearances includes Marie Korchinska, harp, Irene Richards, violin (a member of a distinguished musical family of two brothers and three sisters making up two violins, a viola and two cellos), Gwynne Edwards, viola, and singers Clive Carey, Dennis Noble and Frank Phillips, the last named better known as a BBC announcer.

The 1931/32 season was opened by the then still very young but well established Griller String Quartet playing the Ravel and Mozart K.465 quartets. In the same programme were the two-piano duettists Ethel Bartlett and Rae Robertson. Later in the season Ethel's sister, Edith Bartlett and her husband, Everard de Peyer (parents of Gervase de Peyer) appeared in vocal duets. No fewer than nine piano quintets were performed in this season - Bax, Bloch, Brahms, Dohnanyi, Dvořák, Elgar, Franck, Rheinberger and Schumann and first appearances included pianists Margaret Good and Cyril Smith; violinists Vera Kantrovitch, Alfred Cave and Reginald Morley and cellist Jack Shinebourne.

Yet another piano quintet was played at the opening Concert of the 1932/33 season when a quartet led by Jessie Grimson with Robert Grimson on the cello was joined by another old friend, Johanne Stockmarr, and gave the tenth performance at these Concerts of the piano quintet by the Norwegian composer Sinding. Walthew's works were never absent for long from the programmes and on the second Concert included his setting of

Thackeray's cynical résumé of Goethe's "Sorrows of Werther" sung by Gordon Cleather with the composer at the piano. This favourite among Walthew's songs tells how Charlotte, for love of whom Werther

> "blew his silly brains out . . .
> having seen his body
> Borne before her on a shutter
> Like a well-conducted person,
> Went on cutting bread and butter."

In this same programme Watson Forbes made his first appearance. Later Rae Jenkins, remembered now as conductor of the BBC Midland and Welsh Orchestras, appeared as viola; both were introduced by Isidore Schwiller.

The Canadian Trio, Ida, Sara and Anna Nelson, violin, cello and piano respectively, appeared in December, 1932. Their cellist is now known as Zara Nelsova. Another first appearance was the violinist Jean Pougnet. The season concluded on May 7th, 1933 with a Brahms Centenary Concert, the programme including the C minor piano quartet and the piano quintet. Helen Henschel sang to her own accompaniment several Brahms Lieder. During 1933 all except six of Brahms' concerted chamber works were played. The next season was again opened by the Griller String Quartet. The first work they played was a string quartet by Edric Cundell, later head of the Guildhall School of Music. On December 3rd the entire Concert was given as a piano recital by Myra Hess; Walthew, generous as ever, wrote the special programme notes. On January 7th a Concert was "kindly arranged by Mrs. Ethel Hobday for the extinction of the last season's deficit". This was a family affair in which her husband, Alfred Hobday, played the viola in the two Brahms songs with viola obbligato and her son-in-law, Albert Sammons, played two very well-known violin sonatas, the Brahms in G and the César Franck. Later in the season Schubert's "Trout" quintet was played and this meant that Claude Hobday, (Alfred's brother) was required for the double-bass part. In this performance the pianist was Yvonne Arnaud. The report of the season said: "We are glad that Miss Arnaud's stage and film work have not wholly deprived the musical public of a gifted and accomplished pianist".

1934-1939

Elgar died on the 23rd February, 1934 and a programme of his works was given in his memory on 17th March. The Stratton Quartet played his string quartet and, joined by Harriet Cohen, his piano quintet. Dorothea Webb's songs included the "Sea Pictures" one of the most haunting of Elgar's works.

Frank Merrick, the pianist, made his first appearance on the 8th March with Ernest Tomlinson. They played the Bloch Suite for viola and piano. Later in the season Bloch's piano quintet was given by the Griller Quartet and Freda Swain. The season concluded with a piano recital by Solomon. Other first appearances included Florence Hooton, cellist, and Geoffrey Corbett, pianist, now better known as a conductor.

The Griller quartet once more opened the season of 1934/35 joined by Harry Isaacs in the Bloch piano quintet.

The Concerts have never been well-off. Mr. Clements frequently had to go on to the platform and cajole the audience into putting even more into the collection bowls. In this season Mr. F. Service, on his own behalf and that of two other members of the audience, wrote to the Committee with suggestions for a Guarantee Fund saying that if it was formed they would promise to make regular payments to it over a number of years. In this way the Subscription Fund began - "to enable the Concerts to carry on without being in fear of a deficit" - and it is now an indispensable part of the Concert finances. Later Mr. Service became Honorary Treasurer, a post he held until 1951.

On 11th December, 1934 Isidore Schwiller organised and led another performance of Schönbergs "Verklärte Nacht" which included Lionel Bentley, later the distinguished leader of the Amici Quartet.

Harry Blech commenced a long association with the Concerts on the 16th December, 1934. His quartet then consisted of himself, David Martin, Frederick Riddle and Willem de Mont, all of whom have subsequently played frequently at the Concerts. The young Boyd Neel Orchestra appeared on the 14th April 1935; this consisted of a whole generation of string players whose names have become household words in the musical profession. These first appearances included Samuel Rosenheim (playing the violin, later the viola, who achieved distinction as a conductor before a sudden early death just when he had been appointed conductor of the Jacques Orchestra), Max Gilbert, viola, Peter Beavan, Eileen McCarthy and James Whitehead, cellos, and John Walton, double-bass. The pianist Eileen Joyce played on the 31st March. The last Concert of the season was given by Isidore Schwiller and colleagues and included the Mendelssohn and Svendsen octets.

The opening Concert of the 1935/36 season was given by the Stratton Quartet and it was the first of the Concerts to be broadcast. Walthew wrote about the Concerts in the *Radio Times* of the 4th October. Harry Plunket Greene sang for the last time at these Concerts on the 20th October, his last actual appearance being when he spoke at the Concert in aid of the Musicians' Benevolent Fund on the 19th November. Again one Concert was completely given over to a piano recital, this time by Harold Samuel, a noted interpreter of Bach. Perhaps in deference to Mr. Clements' musical blind-spot this programme contained only one work by Bach. The final Concert of the season, given by the Griller Quartet with Pauline Juler, clarinet and Cyril Smith, piano, included the Mozart clarinet quintet and the Schumann piano quintet and was broadcast. There is an interesting list of first appearances, including pianists Betty Humby (later Lady Beecham), Alan Richardson (known also now as a composer) and Myers Foggin, later the Principal of Trinity College of Music; and the Menges String Quartet.

As a tribute to Plunket Greene who died in 1936 Franklyn Kelsey, one of his pupils, sang at the opening Concert of the 1936/37 season "To the Soul" by Stanford, who had been a lifelong friend of Plunket Greene's. The audience stood as a token of respect. The earlier part of this Concert was given by the Griller String Quartet and was broadcast.

JUBILEE CONCERT

The big event of this season was the Jubilee Concert at the 21st February 1937, the fiftieth anniversary of the first Concert on the 20th February, 1887. A special programme was produced with a picture of A.J. Clements on the front which is reproduced on the frontispiece of this book. This marathon lasted for nearly four hours as meticulously recorded by A.J.C. himself. The artists who appeared at that Concert included the Bessie Rawlins Quartet, Gordon Cleather, Samuel Liddle, Ethel Hobday, Albert Sammons, Helen Henschel, Arthur Alexander, R.H. Walthew, the Griller String Quartet and last but by no means least Alfred J. Clements, who at the request of the Griller Quartet joined them in a quintet by Pierre Haensel (a pupil of Haydn and a contemporary of Beethoven).

Newcomers in this season included cellist Peers Coetmore, pianists Moura Lympany and Phyllis Sellick and violinist Margot McGibbon who played with her pianist husband Frederick Jackson.

The opening Concert of the 1937/38 season was again broadcast - this time the Brosa Quartet together with Walthew playing the Brahms piano quintet. The second Concert of the season was in aid of the Plunket Greene Memorial Fund. In this season piano quintets did very well - the performance of the Brahms was number 35, the César Franck reached its 31st, the Schumann its 41st, the Stanford its 21st and the Dvořák its 43rd and 44th (the Dvořák's present score is 70 and holds the record for number of performances of any single work). There were also played three less well-known quintets: by F. d'Erlanger, Rozycki and Wolf-Ferrari. The Schubert two-cello quintet, oboe quintets by Bax and George Stratton and clarinet quintets by Herbert Howells and Arthur Somervell also featured. Evelyn Rothwell, oboe, made her first appearance in the Bax and Stratton works. Wilfrid Parry played for the first time in the last Concert of the year, on 12th December.

On January 6th, 1938, three days before the first Concert of the second half of the season Alfred J. Clements died aged 79. This tribute, by W.S. Meadmore, written on the occasion of the Jubilee Concert, is perhaps the best possible appreciation of his work:

MR. CLEMENTS WITH THE GRILLER STRING QUARTET
AT HIS JUBILEE CONCERT, 21ST FEBRUARY, 1937

"To most of us Alfred J. Clements and the Concerts are the same thing. From that very first Concert on the 20th February, 1887 he has been the secretary, organiser and the arranger of every Concert presented. There were times when the existence of the Concerts was in jeopardy, their life threatened, their future uncertain; not that Mr. Clements ever admitted this or thought for a moment that the Concerts might come to an end. There were times, many times, in the old South Place days when finance was a weekly worry and the Concerts survived precariously from hand to mouth - it is almost solely due to his energy and enthusiasm that the Concerts have become as they are, something that stands for the best in English musical life. For all these fifty years Mr. Clements has devoted a great deal of what might have otherwise been his leisure to working for the Concerts. Of course, he is a character, one of those truly English eccentrics whom a great Victorian novelist is delighted to depict. The modern generation might consider him altogether an oddity for, utterly devoid of self, has not his greatest happiness been throughout his life the bringing of happiness to other people? I think no one can possibly imagine the time and labour he has always so ungrudgingly given to make the Concerts a success. Nowadays, when music can be heard so easily it is difficult to realise the days when one had to make sacrifices to hear music. But when the South Place Concerts were first started it was no easy matter to hear music in London on Sundays; indeed by many people it was still considered a breaking of the Sabbath. So when the South Place Concerts first started it was something in the nature of a pioneer movement. Under Mr. Clements' guidance they grew to be something much greater - 'the Mecca of all chamber music lovers' as Percy Scholes once wrote . . . it has been Mr. Clements life's work . . . his personality and enthusiasm have inspired musicians to give of their best . . on no single occasion has Mr. Clements ever failed his audience."

Memorials for three artists very much associated with the Concerts have taken the form of in John Saunders' case a scholarship, in Gervase Elwes' case the Musicians' Benevolent Fund and in Plunket Greene's case a private ward for musicians in St. George's Hospital. As a memorial to Mr. Clements it was decided to give an annual prize for a chamber-music work by a British composer. The prize originally £20, has now been raised to £500 and is competed for biennially, the original funds having been augmented by legacies from Mr. Peters (a friend of the Clements) and from Mrs. Clements herself, who died in 1954. The list of prizewinners is in the statistical section of this book. My mother, Mrs. Florence Hawkins, was appointed Honorary Secretary to the fund and held this position for 25 years. Helen Henschel spoke at the inauguration of the fund at the 1300th Concert. The Griller String Quartet, who had played the slow movement of the Dvořák quartet in F Op. 96 at Mr. Clements' cremation, played at this Concert as did Myra Hess. The Quartet was joined by Gerald Moore and Steuart Wilson in a performance of Vaughan Williams' "On Wenlock Edge" song cycle. Apart from the collection at this Concert contributions were received from throughout the musical world, including some from famous musicians who had never played at the Concerts.

The Griller String Quartet again opened the 1938/39 season with Dvořák's E flat quartet and the Elgar piano quintet with Vivian Langrish. Mrs. Dora M. Clements was now Honorary Secretary in succession to her husband and her own view was that the best memorial to her husband was the continuation of the Concerts. Janet Hamilton-Smith sang for the first time this season. Her husband, Gilbert Bailey, who first appeared in 1925 also sang on this occasion. He was a loyal friend to the Concerts and had been a pupil of Harry Plunket Greene. There was a broadcast on the 12th March, 1939 when Katherine Markwell, Pauline Juler and Antonia Butler performed the Brahms trio for piano, clarinet and cello. In the same programme Denis Matthews made his first appearance, as accompanist. Other newcomers were Leonard Hirsch, violinist, and Joan Cross, singer.

The next season, which should have begun on October 1st, 1939 (which was in fact confidently announced on the last programme of the previous season) did not begin then as war was declared on September 3rd. Restrictions on the number of people assembling in central areas prevented any Concerts being given until January 7th, 1940 and then, because of black-out regulations, they were held at 3.0 p.m. until March 7th, when with the longer days it was possible to revert to the customary 6.30 p.m.

The opening Concert was given by the Blech String Quartet with Franz Osborn and included the César Franck piano quintet. Later the first winner of the Clements' Memorial prize, Frederick Durrant, had his prizewinning piano quintet performed by Frank Merrick and the Hirsch quartet and was presented with the prize. Because of the late start there were only seventeen Concerts in this season, though it was extended until May

5th to give the Griller Quartet an opportunity to play after their American tour. They concluded the season with the Mozart D minor quartet K.421, the work which commenced the entire series in 1887 and recommenced them in 1945. There were very few newcomers in this season, presumably because many young musicians had been called up.

The Committee, ever optimistic, hoped to start the Concerts again in the autumn of 1940, but so many members were dispersed it was not until 1945 that they began again.

1945-1969

During the war years the flag of chamber music was kept flying at the National Gallery by the concerts organised by Dame Myra Hess. She was, as previously mentioned, an old friend of the South Place Concerts having first played in 1916. The National Gallery Concerts Trustees produced a book on the occasion of their fifth anniversary very much on the lines of our "Story of a Thousand Concerts", published in 1927. Many of our regular performers played at the National Gallery, notably the Griller String Quartet. They had the distinction of playing at the final concert of the National Gallery series and at our first Concert after the war in October, 1945.

It was a commonplace at the National Gallery Concerts - and in fact at all war-time concerts - for artists to appear in uniform and this practice continued until early 1946 since demobilisation took some time. Whereas a South Place Concert on 18th November, 1917 given by the "Regimental String Quartet of the 31st Battalion Middlesex Regiment" had been dubbed "the Khaki Concert" most of the 1939/45 war and immediate post-war concerts could more accurately be described as "Air Force Blue" concerts. Many of our friends including all the Griller String Quartet, Watson Forbes, Max Gilbert, Leonard Hirsch, Dennis and Leonard Brain, Harry Blech, David Martin, Norman Del Mar, and James Whitehead were in the Central Band of the R.A.F.

Mrs. Clements, who had taken over the secretaryship when her husband died, was now 80. Her indomitable spirit and determination to carry on the life's work of her husband overcame the difficulties of a fresh start and on October 7th, 1945 the first post-war Concert was given.

There were many changes. Money had fallen in value, costs in running the Concerts had increased and it was soon realised that a collection was no longer sufficient to meet post-war expenses. The Committee reluctantly faced the need to abandon the free admission with silver collection which had been a feature of the Concerts since they started in 1887. But we still determined to keep the spirit of their original aim, that no one should be prevented from attending for financial reasons. Some free seats were kept, but generally the admission charge would be one shilling. Even this would not cover costs, but the Arts Council gave us a grant. Singers were no longer a regular part of every programme and the printed programme itself became austere with no notes nor words of songs, but incidentally cheaper in price - ld. Programme policy has not changed from then up to the present day but costs have, so that the admission charges have slowly increased in line with inflation. But from 1952 season tickets were introduced which cut the price in half for regular South Place concert goers.

On October 7th, 1945 the Griller String Quartet, as already mentioned, gave the long awaited opening Concert of the first season after the break due to the war. The programme was the Mozart in D minor K.421, Brahms B flat and Haydn Op. 33 No. 3. It is to our very great regret that they were not to play for us again.

Four established string quartet teams appeared for us in this and subsequent seasons - three of them had appeared before but all of them had changed their personnel: the Blech and Hirsch retained their leaders only and the Aeolian (formerly the Stratton) their viola and cello. As the report of the season sadly records neither Carl Taylor (2nd violin of the Stratton) nor Douglas Thomson (viola of the Blech) had survived the war. The fourth team was a quartet which had been formed during the war, a ladies' quartet led by Olive Zorian, with Marjorie Lavers, Winifred Copperwheat and Norina Semino. These last two had previously played at the Concerts. Their first appearance was interesting in that they played for the first time at these Concerts Michael Tippett's 2nd quartet, introduced from the platform by Walter Bergmann to whom the work is dedicated. Earlier in the afternoon this work had been played at the Wigmore Hall by the Amsterdam Quartet and the Zorian Quartet had listened to it; the Amsterdam Quartet returned the compliment and came to Conway Hall to hear the Zorian's performance. The Rawlins and the Menges Quartets, both of whom had played before the war, reappeared. The Menges Quartet played Vaughan Williams' A minor quartet "For Jean on her Birthday"; this is the quartet with a very important viola part, played on this occasion by Jean Stewart, to whom the work is dedicated. First appearances included violinists Maria Lidka, Felix Kok and Colin Sauer (later leader of the Dartington Quartet), Vivian Joseph, cello, and singers Robert Irwin and René Soames.

The winter of 1946/47 was the severest in living memory and financially this was the most disastrous to date - the deficit amounted to nearly £135. Two more regular quartet teams joined us: the Martin and Hurwitz quartets. The Hurwitz were all newcomers to the Concerts. Three of the Martin were old friends but Neville Marriner, their second violin, was playing for us for the first time. The Martin Quartet played the "Biscay" quartet of McEwen who was then still alive and had advised them during rehearsals.

The 1400th Concert which fell on the sixtieth anniversary was given on 23rd February, 1947 and was celebrated by a performance of the Schubert Octet, in which Norman del Mar, now famous as a conductor, made his first appearance playing the horn. Walthew, in programme notes specially written for the occasion, pointed out that Alfred J. Clements "had a special affection for Schubert's music and for this Octet in particular". Not only were Walthew's notes a special feature but the entire programme was set up typographically to simulate a pre-war one.

At the end of the 1946/47 season Mrs. Clements retired as Secretary. She was 82 and had been associated with the Concerts for sixty years. She had gallantly maintained the running of the Concerts since the death of her husband but increasing infirmity meant that she now had to give up. George Hutchinson, who had joined the Concert Committee in 1930, becoming assistant secretary in 1932, now took over the secretaryship.

In the 1947/48 season the financial crisis of the previous year was overcome by reducing the number of artists throughout the season and concentrating on string quartets. There was also a higher average attendance figure for each Concert. This season coincided with the fiftieth anniversary of Brahms' death and we set out to perform all his string quartets, the piano quintet and as many of his other chamber music works as possible. The quartets were performed by the Hurwitz Quartet, joined in the piano quintet by Kyla Greenbaum whose father had been a member of the famous Brosa quartet. Antonio Brosa himself gave a violin recital which included the D minor sonata. Another ensemble which commenced a long association with the Concerts in this season was the Robert Masters piano quartet (Robert Masters, violin, Nannie Jamieson, viola, Muriel Taylor, cello, Kinloch Anderson, piano).

We had rather a surprise on February 29th, 1948 when a new quartet filled the hall, including all the standing room, to capacity. The quartet had only just chosen the name Amadeus (earlier South Place publicity had described it as the Brainin Quartet). This was, I believe their second major public performance, the first having been at the Wigmore Hall where also the "House Full" notices went out. The Concerts are what they are because such teams have played for us in their early days and are still willing to play for us even when they are internationally famous.

During this season there was a special Schubert Concert at which the first complete performance in the history of the Concerts of the song cyle "Winterreise" was given by Victor Carne. There were also two pianist newcomers - the distinguished composer Edmund Rubbra and Colin Horsley.

Ingpen and Williams, the Concert Agency, made it possible for us to secure the services of some very distinguished foreign artists for the 1948/49 season. The first to appear under this arrangement was the Loewenguth quartet, from France, who opened the season. Apart from quartets by Haydn and Dvořák they also played an early work by their own second violinist, Jacques Murgier. The famous tenor Julius Patzak sang "Die Schöne Müllerin" on 10th October.

An omission to which Meadmore draws attention in "The Story of a Thousand Concerts" was made good on 12th December by the Aeolian Quartet who gave the first performance at the Concerts of Beethoven's "Grosse Fuge" Op. 133.

There were two orchestral Concerts this season, one of them a varied programme of very old and very new music given by the Morley College String Orchestra conducted by Matyas Seiber in which Sophie Wyss and Norbert Brainin appeared as soloists. The other orchestral Concert was given by the Informal Chamber Orchestra in which John Cruft, later Music Director of the Arts Council, was soloist in the Strauss oboe concerto. Dennis Brain made his first two appearances at the Concerts, on the second occasion with his wind ensemble playing the Clements Memorial prizewinning work, a wind quintet by his schoolfriend, Racine Fricker. It was this work, aided by this performance, which helped to establish Racine Fricker as a composer. Other first appearances include Sidney Sutcliffe, oboe, Henry Holst, violin, and J.W. Merrett, double-bass, son of an equally famous double-bass player, J.E. Merrett (1946/47).

BARTÓK

The most striking event in the 1949-50 season was the performance of all six Bartók String Quartets, the first time the six had been played in London on a public platform in one series. Many difficulties had to be overcome to make their presentation possible, for few teams had Bartók in their repertoire and scores and parts of some of the quartets, not then available here, had to be obtained by devious means from abroad. Up to our Centenary Concert number one will have been played fifteen times, number two twenty times, number three seventeen times, numbers four and five fourteen times and number six twenty times.

Rudolf Schock sang at a Concert to celebrate Goethe's bicentenary on November 20th. Two new quartets appeared for the first time: the Aleph, led by Alan Loveday, and the Peter Gibbs (with Kelly Isaacs, Patrick Ireland and James Christie) who included Bloch's second quartet in their first Concert. The orchestral Concert was given by the Riddick String Orchestra, again with Sophie Wyss as soloist. The famous cellist Maurice Eisenberg, joined with Frederick Thurston and Harold Craxton in the Brahms trio. On March 26th Bach's "Art of Fugue" was performed for the first time at these Concerts. This was in the arrangement by Watson Forbes (who also played) for violin, viola, cello and viola da gamba - a most successful arrangement of this work for four players. It has been repeated three times since but with a cello replacing the gamba.

The list of newcomers to the Concerts in this season is extensive: apart from those already mentioned it includes: - clarinet - Jack Brymer; violins - Tessa Robbins, Hugh Bean, Erich Gruenberg, Patrick Halling, Granville Jones, Manoug Parikian; violas - Cecil Aronowitz, Stephen Shingles, Marjorie Lempfert; cellos - Francisco Gabarro, Peter Halling.

The 1950/51 season was one of the most successful in our history with an average attendance of 428 (seating capacity of Conway Hall is 501). All Beethoven's quartets and the major chamber works of Bloch were given with three exceptions. From abroad came the Barylli and Vegh Quartets who each included a Beethoven quartet. The Vegh, well known for their Bartók performances, also played Bartók's 4th quartet.

Most of the Bloch works had extensive programme notes by Alex Cohen; he was a great admirer of Bloch's works and had studied them closely. In particular the Peter Gibbs Quartet got much assistance from him in their preparation. He was a gentle, cultured man whose interests outside music (he had been leader of the Birmingham Orchestra) included translating French poetry.

The New London Quartet (successor to the Blech, now led by Erich Gruenberg) gave the 1500th Concert on December 10th, 1950. We used the old pre-war lay-out of the programme which was no problem especially since we had the same printer with some of the same staff. Mr. Clements, as a retired printer, preserved the blocks of the programme notes and used them again and again. We used two programme notes first used in 1888 and 1889. The note on the Dvořák piano quintet, composed 1887, began: "One of the finest of modern quintets . . ."!

Beethoven's quartet Op. 130 in its original version with the Grosse Fuge Op. 133 as its last movement was given for the first time in this way at these Concerts on February 11th by the Aeolian String Quartet. Alan Loveday, as well as his appearances in the Aleph Quartet, also appeared in an all-Bloch programme with a piano trio introducing two newcomers, Peggy Gray, piano, and Amaryllis Fleming, cello.

The Aeolian Quartet opened the 1951/52 season playing Franz Reizenstein's piano quintet with the composer at the piano. Murray Dickie sang "Die Schöne Müllerin". The only foreign quartet to play this season was the Koeckert who played a work by Krenek (the pill, as usual, was surrounded by jam in the form of Beethoven and Schubert). The Amadeus Quartet joined by Cecil Aronowitz played a Mozart programme (anniversary conscious as usual, the 160th of Mozart's death). Gareth Morris played in a programme of works which were nearly all new to the Concerts - including Debussy's sonata for flute, viola and harp (in which he was joined by Watson Forbes and Gwendolen Mason) and, surprisingly, one of Mozart's flute quartets. In this season Martin Lincé became honorary treasurer, a post he still holds.

The London Harpsichord Ensemble including John Francis, flute, and Millicent Silver, harpsichord, played on April 20th and two pianists made their first appearances: Iris Loveridge and Mewton-Wood.

In the 1952/53 season the ten celebrated Mozart, all the middle and late Beethoven (except Ops. 127 and 133) and all the six Bartók string quartets were given. Three foreign quartets played for us - the Manoliu (Swiss), the Röntgen and the Dutch (both from Holland). There were last-minute alterations due to illness on three occasions; twice, when members of quartets became ill the situation was saved by the Harry Isaacs piano trio. The Tippett song cycle, "The Heart's Assurance", which was to have been sung by Thorstein Hanneson was given very successfully at short notice by Amy Shuard, with John Gardner at the piano. The orchestral Concert was again given by the Riddick String Orchestra. Pianist Peter Katin played for the first time.

The interest aroused by the Röntgen's performance of Pijper's quartet no. 4 in the previous season was such that we arranged to play all five Pijper quartets in the 1953/54 season, the Röntgen repeating no. 4. Subsequently these quartets were broadcast. Lengnick's, the publishers of Pijper, hastened their publication of one of his quartets to make this series possible. The other foreign quartets to play were the Benthien and the Dutch. It is to our regret that this was the last season in which we were able to engage foreign artists. Ilse Wolf sang for the first time in this season. In her programme she was joined by Gervase de Peyer and Cyril Preedy in Schubert's "Der Hirt auf dem Felsen", a work which had been performed only twice previously at the Concerts. In subsequent Concerts she has now sung this work for us nine times.

The severe smog of December, 1952, had reduced the audience for the Trout quintet played by the Robert Masters piano quartet and J. Edward Merrett to a brave two hundred; the identical programme was given again this season to a full house. Again, making good last season's loss, Thorstein Hanneson did sing Tippett's "The Heart's Assurance". The Melos Ensemble (Goren, McMahon, Aronowitz, Weil, Beers, de Peyer, Draper, Saunders) appeared for the first time on January 10th playing the Beethoven septet and the Schubert octet as did the Allegri Quartet (Eli Goren, James Barton, Patrick Ireland and William Pleeth) on February 7th.

The singer Margaret Ritchie made an appearance in this season; this was an interesting link with the past as she was probably the last pupil of Plunket Greene to sing at the Concerts.

There is again a long list of newcomers; apart from those mentioned above it includes: violins - Sylvia Cleaver, Trevor Williams, Carl Pini; violas - Margaret Major, Harold Harriott; cellos - Anna Shuttleworth, Norman Jones; pianos - Eric Harrison, Martin Isepp, Clive Lythgoe, Peter Gellhorn.

In the 1954/55 season all the Beethoven and Dvořák string quintets were played - The Hirsch String Quartet opened the season with an all-Beethoven programme.

Iso Elinson played Beethoven's "Hammerklavier" sonata; both this work and its player were new to the Concerts. In the same programme Alexander Young gave a superb performance of Schumann's "Dichterliebe". This was the first of several annual appearances in which he sang for us many important works: "Die Schöne Müllerin", "Winterreise", Schumann's "Liederkreis von Heine", Britten's "Holy Sonnets of John Donne", "Winter Words" and "Michelangelo Sonnets", Schubert's "Schwanengesang". Mr. Young specially prepared many of these recitals for us. They represented for him first performances in public of the great song cycles, and critics and public alike acclaimed his outstanding success in this relatively new role as Lieder singer.

Mention should be made here of the change in policy regarding singers: whereas before the war a singer appeared in nearly every programme, public taste and financial considerations dictated that singers should appear once or twice a season only, and when they did appear they should sustain all or the main part of the programme, usually with a complete song cycle.

Schönberg's "Verklärte Nacht" was played this season by the Hirsch String Quartet with Watson Forbes and Christopher Bunting. It had last been played 20 years previously with Isidore Schwiller as leader. Mr. Forbes had played on the previous occasion also.

Much new music was introduced to the public for the first time: Iain Hamilton's (a Clements prizewinner) clarinet and piano sonata, Fricker's horn and piano sonata, Rawsthorne's 2nd and Bloch's 4th string quartets. The Wang String Quartet (later the University Ensemble) played for us for the first time, as did the Hurwitz Chamber Ensemble, whose programme included the Vivaldi concerto for four violins.

On October 16th Mrs. Dora M. Clements died in her ninetieth year.

The season 1955/56 in which the 200th anniversary of Mozart's birth occurred was celebrated with much of his music:

a horn concerto, a symphony, a wind ensemble work, two 2-horn sextets, the clarinet quintet, three string quintets, the horn quintet, eleven string quartets, the two flute quartets, the two piano quartets, the oboe quartet, two piano trios, one string trio, one violin and viola duet and a piano sonata for four hands.

The orchestral Concert this season was given by the Dennis Brain Chamber Orchestra. As well as conducting, Dennis played the Mozart horn concerto K.447. This supreme horn player was never to play for us again; he was killed in a motor accident the following year at the early age of thirty-seven. His brother, Leonard, played the Fricker concertante for cor anglais and strings. Earlier in the season the distinguished oboist, Leon Goossens, played the Mozart and Arnold Cooke oboe quartets with the Carter String Trio; it is interesting that this was his first appearance with us, though his first public appearance was before the First War.

Another attempt to play all six Bartók quartets was made in the 1956/57 season but it was unsuccessful, only numbers 1, 2 and 3 reaching the platform. The newly-formed Amici Quartet (led by Lionel Bentley, an old friend who had been in the Blech and New London Quartets) played no. 3, the most formidable of the six. Their first appearance with us fell on the seventieth anniversary of the Concerts. Another quartet, new to us was the New Edinburgh. John Moore, cellist, who had for years been in the Aeolian, previously the Stratton Quartet, retired and Derek Simpson took his place. Again the Orchestral Concert was given by the Hurwitz Ensemble. Yfrah Neaman, violin, Christopher Martin, viola, and Joan Dickson, cello, played for us for the first time.

During 1957/58 we prevailed upon the Amici Quartet's friendliness (as we have continued to do) to the extent of having them play four times in the season, including both the opening and the final Concert, which was given in aid of the Musicians' Benevolent Fund. On this later occasion they were joined by Thea King in the Brahms clarinet quintet. We successfully brought to the platform Bartók's 4th, 5th and 6th quartets, left out of our plans for the previous season. There were five Concerts by different piano teams which meant that fifteen different piano trios were heard, all from the standard repertoire. Celia Arieli, piano, made her first appearance in one of these trios. A very fine new team - the Prometheus Ensemble - performed the Spohr Nonet and the Schubert Octet. Alan Civil, horn, and Gwydion Brooke, bassoon, were among players in this ensemble new to us.

There were several special features about the 1958/59 season - one was the first broadcast for twenty years (actually a pre-recording subsequently broadcast) which took place at the Concert on October 19th. The performers, Margaret Good and William Pleeth, were introduced by Robert Irwin, who had sung for us several times in the past. The other was the performance of all six Bartók quartets by the Amici, thus becoming the first team to play all the six Bartók quartets in London in one season. It would take another quartet team to understand what such a feat implies, for this was a series of performances based on a fine technique and a true understanding of the Bartók idiom and involving many hours of intensive study and rehearsal. South Place Concerts are very happy to have provided a platform for such an important event in London's musical history. The players were Lionel Bentley, Sylvia Cleaver, Harold Harriott and Joy Hall. Steven Staryk, violin, and Adela Kotowska, piano, gave one of the most outstanding sonata recitals we have had.

At the final Concert of the season, given by the London String Quartet, Ivor James spoke in aid of the Musicians' Benevolent Fund. Appeal speakers sometimes go on at length and so did he; but - this delightful personality could never speak too much for me. Newcomers this season include John Tunnell, violin; Peter Wallfisch, piano; Reginald Kell, clarinet.

The 1959/60 season opened with the Amadeus Quartet with the characteristic (post-war) South Place programme of Haydn-Bartók-Brahms. Most of our familiar quartet teams played for us and in particular on November 19th, 1959, the Hirsch and Amici quartets co-operated in performances of the Mendelssohn octet and the Brahms B flat sextet and the Mozart E flat quintet. The Virtuoso Ensemble made two appearances, on one of them playing the Schubert octet and the Beethoven septet. When the secretary spoke to Ilse Wolf about a desire to have a performance of Brahms' Liebeslieder she offered to organise one and triumphantly surmounting the great difficulties involved got together a superb team: herself, Janet Baker, Edgar Fleet and John Shirley-Quirk, with Kinloch Anderson and Bernice Lehmann at the piano. With such a team it was a thrilling and delightful performance. It had last been done twenty-two years previously by Miriam Licette, Dorothy Clark, John McKenna and Vere Laurie with Gerald Moore and George Reeves.

Ilse Wolf sang again during this season, taking the place of Alexander Young at short notice because of his illness. She was able to sing much of his original programme. The Hurwitz Chamber Ensemble again gave the orchestral Concert. Colin Horsley and the Amici played the Brahms quintet and by happy coincidence, in every season since, they have played a piano quintet.

The English String Quartet (Nona Liddell, Eleanor St. George, Marjorie Lempfert - daughter of Marjorie Hayward mentioned earlier - and Helen Just) made their first appearance as a team, though most of them had previously appeared individually. Other newcomers were violinists Hugh Maguire and Kenneth Sillito. Colin Mason wrote an article on the Concerts in *The Guardian* of October 15th headed "Seventy Years of Chamber Music". His conclusion was "They (the Concerts) have ceased to be a social institution on the fringe of London's musical life, and have become instead, as the only regular series of concerts where Londoners can hear the classical chamber music repertory, a musical institution essential to the completeness of that life".

The Colin Horsley-Amici partnership opened the 1960/61 season with the forty-eighth performance of the Schumann piano quintet. It was planned to include all the Schönberg and the first six Shostakovich quartets but due to ill-luck Schönberg 1 and Shostakovich 6 could not be fitted in. Schönberg 2 had a narrow escape; it has an exacting vocal part and the singer was taken ill a few hours before the Concert. Dorothy Dorow sang this part, practically at sight, and was acclaimed next day in the press.

It is always surprising to find a classical work which has not been performed at the Concerts - two Haydn quartets which had slipped through Mr. Clements' net were played for the first time this season. There were two orchestral Concerts, one by the Hurwitz Ensemble, the other by the Hirsch Chamber Players. The Dumka Piano Trio, a team new to the Concerts, gave the Musicians' Benevolent Fund Concert, and the Oromonte String Trio also appeared for the first time. Other newcomers included Janet Craxton, oboe; Barry Tuckwell, horn; and David Galliver, tenor.

In the next season the two quartets missing from our previous season's attempted complete series of Schönberg and Shostakovich were played. The Dartington Quartet commenced their association with us on November 5th, 1961. The Portia Wind Ensemble, a ladies team, had the last word with the final Concert of the season playing three works new to the Concerts - the Mozart E flat and the Hugo Cole wind octet and the Dvořák Serenade for wind, cello and double-bass.

The exceptionally severe winter of the 1962/63 season affected attendances drastically, but the smaller audiences enjoyed Concerts as good as any we had had before. The re-formed Edinburgh Quartet made its first appearance for us. This team included two names that have long and happy associations with the Concerts. The second violin, Julian Cummings, was the son of Keith Cummings of the London String Quartet and Ian Hampton, cello, the son of Colin Hampton, the cellist of the Griller Quartet. The Dartington String Quartet with newcomer Penelope Howard (now leader of the Arriaga String Quartet) playing second viola played the Mozart C and the Brahms G quintets. The other Brahms quintet, in F, was played by the English String Quartet, with John Yewe Dyer making a welcome reappearance for the first time since before the war. Quintin Ballardie with the Hurwitz Chamber Ensemble played the Telemann concerto in G for viola and Mavis Elmitt with the Hirsch Chamber Players played the Bach D minor piano concerto. These two orchestras contained many of the finest London string players.

Newcomers included also Josef Weingarten piano; William Bennett, flute; Keith Harvey, cello.

Because of the previous season's severe deficit of nearly three hundred pounds, even after taking into account the generous subsidy from the South Place Ethical Society and the Arts Council, we had a good look at the way we ran the Concerts in the 1963/64 season. A questionnaire revealed that most of the audience like our present type of programme and that our most economic advertisement is by leaflet distribution, either personal or by mailing list. We also found that people were happy with the six-thirty start, a time that also had been decided many years ago by questionnaire. In fact there was little we could change; we just had to hope that better weather would encourage the audiences that our programmes merited.

Another first appearance this season was coffee in the interval for the audience! By popular demand it has appeared at every concert since.

A fine new quartet - the Alberni - played for us this season. They had been coached by Sidney Griller and are supported by Harlow New Town.

During 1964/65 we aimed to have the Aeolian String Quartet play the six Bartók and to include in the programmes all the Beethoven and Brahms string quartets. We succeeded in all but the Bartók series. Watson Forbes took up a BBC appointment in Glasgow in January after 94 appearances at the Concerts over 32 years. Margaret Major replaced him as violist in the quartet. This meant that the Aeolian could only do one to four, but the Amici and the Edinburgh came to the rescue by playing five and six respectively. The season ended with a performance of the Schubert octet by the Melos Ensemble at which William Waterhouse, bassoon, made his first appearance.

Another first for us in chamber music records was the performance in the 1965/66 season of the first ten Shostakovich quartets. Numbers 9 and 10, played by the Alberni, were also having their first public performance in this country. The music of these quartets, not available here, was brought over at Benjamin Britten's suggestion by Rostropovich, the famous cellist. The Arriaga Quartet made their first appearance for us on January 30th including Tippett's second quartet in their programme. The Amici and Martin Quartets combined on February

27th to give a first South Place performance of an octet by the nineteenth-century composer, Raff, and two pieces for string octet by Shostakovich. Naturally they concluded with the Mendelssohn octet (which was *not* a South Place first - in fact the twentieth!).

On February 2nd, 1967, my mother died. She had been on the Committee since 1922, and since 1945 assistant honorary secretary. A fortnight earlier "Fol" - Miss F.J. Simons - also died. She first joined the Committee in 1914, though her service was not unbroken. She was to be found at the bookstall in the entrance hall right up to the week before her death.

In this season, 1966/67, there were no newcomers in the quartet teams but there were two new piano trios - the Oromonte, with the pianist, Nina Milkina, appearing for the first time, and the Tunnell, consisting of two brothers and a sister, Charles (cello) and Susan (piano) making first appearances. The Dartington Quartet played the Dvořák A major sextet; the second cello, Gillian Steel, was a newcomer. Neil Black, oboe; Keith Puddy, clarinet; John Gray, double-bass; Derek Hammond-Stroud, baritone. all came for the first time.

The 1967/68 season began with the re-formed London String Quartet playing Beethoven. Most of Brahms' chamber music was played during the season. There was one programme of violin sonatas (Beethoven, Bartók and Brahms) given by Raymond Cohen and Anthya Rael, appearing for the first time. Desmond Dupré had the distinction of being the first guitarist to appear on our platform. He played, with the Hurwitz String Trio, the Schubert guitar quartet. Barry Tuckwell, horn, and newcomers Margaret Kitchin, piano, and Galina Solochin joined forces in the twentieth performance of the Brahms horn trio. At the end of the season the youthful Camerata String Orchestra gave an excellent Concert which included the Bartók Divertimento and, with Thea King as soloist, the Stamitz clarinet concerto.

Eileen Croxford, cello, played for the first time and the list of newcomers is considerable because of the Camerata's personnel.

The 1968/69 season included our 2,000th Concert. It was given in the Queen Elizabeth Hall (Conway Hall being too small for the anticipated audience - in fact there was a full house) by the Amadeus String Quartet and Gervase de Peyer. The programme was the Haydn G minor quartet Op. 74 No. 3, Beethoven F Op. 135 and the Mozart clarinet quintet. The concert was broadcast; it was also our annual Musicians' Benevolent Fund Concert for which the artists always give their services. The annual report records that "the months of preparation were rewarded by an extremely enjoyable and successful evening." In addition to Gervase de Peyer three other distinguished clarinettists played during the course of the season: Sidney Fell with the Virtuoso Ensemble, Thea King with the Dartington String Quartet and Jack Brymer. The latter joined with Ilse Wolf and Wilfrid Parry in Schubert's "Der Hirt auf dem Felsen." We tried to include, once again, all the Bartók, Beethoven and the ten celebrated Mozart string quartets but were prevented from doing so by illness. However, in the Clements tradition every Sunday during the season had its concert and the Arriaga, Dartington, Georgian and Martin String Quartets provided excellent substitute programmes. Among the newcomers was Bernard Roberts.

Despite the excellent standards of the previous season the attendances in 1969/70 were not as high as usual. One notices this fluctuation when going through the Concerts season by season; it is always hard to pinpoint the cause; it is not necessarily the weather (the winter of 1968/69 was mild). An impresario who could fathom this could be likened to a doctor who had found the elixir of life!

We made good the promises of Bartók, Beethoven and Mozart string quartets from the previous season and in fact not a single programme had to be changed through illness. Piano trios and piano quintets were featured this season: 16 trios and five of the greatest quintets: Bloch, Brahms, Dvořák, Schumann and Shostakovich.

A partnership with us, which happily still continues, began in this season with the first appearance of brother and sister Ian Partridge (tenor) and Jennifer Partridge (piano). On this occasion they performed Schumann's song cycle "Dichterliebe". A programme of wind music on December 14th by the Northern Sinfonia Ensemble included the Dvořák Wind Serenade (played here only once before, in 1962) and also first performances (for us) of works by Gounod, Françaix and Janaček. Newcomer (as horn player with the Northern Sinfonia): Frank Hawkins.

During the 1970/71 season the eight Dvorák and the five Bloch string quartets were played. The Lindsay Quartet (Peter Cropper, Michael Adamson, Roger Bigley and Bernard Gregor-Smith) played for us for the first time, once in the normal course of events and then the following week for the Musicians' Benevolent Fund Concert they stood in for the Gabrieli Quartet who had been billed to play.

Between the concerts on February 7th and 14th the price of the programme changed in name from sixpence (i.e. 6d.) to 2½p; the admission charge had now reached 4/- (20p).

Among the newcomers to our platform were Marisa Robles, Christopher Hyde-Smith, Mary Ryan, Benjamin Luxon and the Lindsay String Quartet (already mentioned).

In the 1971/72 season we set out to play Shostakovich quartets Nos. 1 - 12 but were unable to manage No. 3. Also featured were important string sextets and quintets. We very much appreciated the dedicated hard work of Trevor Williams and Mary Ryan who prepared Bach's Art of Fugue for a manageable chamber music ensemble, performed it with the rest of their colleagues in the Tilford Festival Players, and provided programme notes. This excellent transcription has been used for each subsequent performance right up to the present day. This work had last been performed in 1962 in a version by Watson Forbes which was no longer available after his retirement.

Three new string quartets appeared: the Chilingirian (Levon Chilingirian, Mark Butler, Simon Rowland-Jones, Philip de Groote); the Jupiter (Homi Kanga, Ernest Scott, Rachel Godlee, James Christie); and the Cummings (Diana Cummings, Julian Cummings, Luciano Jorio, Douglas Cummings).

On February 20th the hall was in near darkness due to a power cut through industrial action. We managed as best we could (we had to forgo coffee) with the obligatory secondary lighting circuit augmented by a light run from a car battery so that the ticket sellers could see the money! Ian Partridge with his sister Jennifer gave a performance of Schubert's "Winterreise" song cycle. I, for one, was glad of the darkness as I was so moved that the tears streamed down my face.

Once again in the 1972/73 season all Bartók string quartets were played, also the Beethoven and Schumann and six important piano quintets (Brahms, Dvořák, Elgar, Franck, Schumann and Shostakovich). For the first time since the Amici in 1958/59 all six Bartók were played by the same team, this time the Georgian, and in chronological order coupled with the late Beethoven and Haydn Op. 20 Nos. one to six.

There was a record of fourteen different string quartet teams: new were the Carl Pini (Carl Pini, Gordon Bennett, John Gould, Barbara Woolley); the Fitzwilliam (Nicholas Dowding, John Phillips, Alan George, Ioan Davies); and the Sartori (Christopher Rowland, Roland Fudge, Philip Clark, Robert Glenton).

Continuing their good work after their previous season's success with Bach's "Art of Fugue" the Tilford Festival Players played Bach's "Musical Offering".

The Northern Sinfonia Ensemble played again - an entire programme of works new to the Concerts, not so surprising in the case of Villa-Lobos and D'Indy, but at last a performance of Mozart's Serenade K361 for thirteen wind.

The published aim in the 1973/74 season was to have a good cross-section of Mozart's chamber music. Twenty-seven of his works were played including the ten famous string quartets, both the violin and viola duos, the clarinet-viola-piano trio, the Adagio for cor anglais and strings, the horn quintet and the piano and wind quintet. Not played was the Divertimento for string trio, to take place in the next season. Not advertised was an attempt to have as many woodwind works as possible. This produced some remarkably varied programmes which included the Ravel Septet. The Medici String Quartet (Paul Robertson, David Matthews, Paul Silverthorne, Antony Lewis) played for us for the first time, also Janet Hilton (clarinet), Timothy Brown (horn), Ifor James (horn) and John McCaw (clarinet).

In 1974/75 a representative selection of Schubert's chamber music was featured; all the Mendelssohn string quartets were played, also nine twentieth century British string quartets. Berkeley, David Blake, Alan Bush, Elgar, Maconchy, Rawsthorne, Seiber, Tippett, Walton.

For the first time at the Concerts Spohr's wind and string octet was played, by the Northern Sinfonia Ensemble, and also Stravinsky's "Pierrot Lunaire", with Lissa Gray and the Tilford Ensemble. There were many new names from the Northern Sinfonia and other newcomers included Ian Brown (piano) and the young cellist Thomas Igloi, who sadly died a year or so later. The Amici Quartet reappeared in the form of Lionel Bentley, John Trusler, Robert Hope Simpson and Bernard Richards.

We began the 1975/76 season with the sad news of the untimely death of Sylvia Cleaver, who had had an association with the Concerts since 1953. She had played in all six of the Bartók quartets as second violin of the Amici Quartet in 1958 and again as leader of the Georgian Quartet in 1972. This was the quartet she lead from 1968 until her death, with numerous appearances at Conway Hall playing most of the greatest chamber music works.

Most of Brahms' chamber music was played this season and all the six Bartók string quartets; the Amici Quartet played Nos. 1, 5 & 6. The Art of Fugue was played again by the Tilford Festival Ensemble. A new string quartet, the Rasoumovsky (Simon Standage, Mary Eade, Simon Whistler and Joanna Milholland) played, and a new ensemble with old instruments, the Jaye Consort of Viols.

Three significant works received their first South Place Sunday Concerts performance in the 1976/77 season: the last Shostakovich string quartet, No. 15, by the Fitzwilliam String Quartet; the Bax piano quintet ("an unjustly neglected work" [illegible]e annual report says) played by Colin Horsley and the [illegible]nci String Quartet; and Messiaen's "Quatuor pour la Fin du Temps", a work we had wanted for some time, played by the Meridian Ensemble. Many pieces either for woodwind alone or for woodwind with strings were played thus introducing a considerable number of new faces. A new cellist, Robert Cohen, played in a trio with his parents, Raymond Cohen and Anthea Rael.

In the 1977/78 season there was a significant increase in the number of people attending the Concerts. In the previous season we had reported a fall-off in attendance. We appealed to the audience (not for the first time) to:

Talk about us to your friends
Send us names for our mailing list
Give leaflets to chamber music lovers
Display a poster

This evidently worked, as 1,188 more people came to the Concerts this season - an increase of 18 per cent. Our programmes maintained their standards. The accent was on Dvořák, Bloch, Britten and Tippett. The season began with the Allegri-Robles Ensemble who not only played the Ravel Septet (the Introduction and Allegro for flute, clarinet, harp and string quartet) but also gave the first performance for us of a work for the same combination of instruments written for and dedicated to their ensemble by Stephen Dodgson. The Tilford Ensemble repeated Bach's "Musical Offering".

This season's new quartets were the Bochmann: Michael Bochmann, David Angel, Gustav Clarkson and Sebastian Comberti, and the Coull: Roger Coull, Philip Gallaway, David Curtis and Martin Thomas.

In 1978/79 our intention was to perform all the Beethoven, Bartók and the ten celebrated Mozart. We succeeded except for the Mozart D minor and Bartók No. 2, which the Dartington could not manage because of illness. This was made good in the next season.

On November 26th The King's Musick gave us a programme of music by composers who lived in the 16th, 17th and early 18th century, an interesting change from our usual fare.

Three new string quartets played for us: the Court: Andrew Court, Elizabeth Partridge, Ian Pearson, Martin Bradshaw; the Quartet of London: Rolf Wilson, Ita Herbert, Graeme Scott, Peter Willison; the Arioso: Jeremy Ballard, Eleanor Cooke, Gwyn Williams, Simon Clugston.

All the important chamber music works of Brahms and Mendelssohn were featured in the 1979/80 season. The Annual Report regrets that, although "inevitably and delightfully many of Haydn's string quartets were included" in all our (then) 93 years we have still not managed to include all he has written.

At the risk of excessive repetition it should be mentioned again that our old friends, the Tilford Ensemble, played Bach's "Art of Fugue" again, and the Allegri-Robles Ensemble the Ravel Septet. Alan Hacker played for us for the first time, playing clarinet in the Brahms clarinet quintet and basset clarinet in two little-known works of Mozart, also new to the Concerts. Three new quartet teams appeared for the first time: the London: Carl Pini, Benedict Cruft, Rusen Gunes, Roger Smith; the Guadagnini: Jennifer Nickson, Julie Taylor, Richard Muncey, John Chillingworth; the Hanson: Peter Hanson, Stephen Rouse, Peter Lale, Martin Loveday.

In the 1980/81 season our attempt to get the four Schönberg string quartets played failed in respect of No. 3. Regrettably this failure was not made good in the following season. However, all the Beethoven string quartets were played, as intended. Once upon a time the number of fingers on one hand was enough to count the string quartet teams who played on the South Place Sunday Concerts' platform. Both hands are now required (also a few toes!). All our old friends reappeared plus the Endellion: Andrew Watkinson, Louise Williams, Garfield Jackson, David Waterman; and the Locrian: Andrew Laing, Gordon Buchan, Timothy Grant, Justin Pearson.

All the Bartók and a good selection of the Mozart string quartets were played in the 1981/82 season. Two new quartet teams: the Amphion: Adrian Levine, Colin Callow, Stephen Tees, Michael Hurwitz; and the Newcastle: Barry Wilde, Clive Lander, Andrew Williams, Jeannette Mountain. The Concerts' parent society, South Place Ethical Society, successfully fought an expensive legal case concerning its claim to charitable status. Judge Dillon made special reference to the Concerts in his judgment: "As I see it, a sentiment or attitude of mind founded in reason can only be cultivated or encouraged to grow by educational methods, including music, and the appreciation of music by performances of high quality." To help defray the costs an appeal was made, and audience, artists and other well-wishers contributed £1,140.11.

The emphasis in the 1982/83 season was on Schumann, Shostakovich string quartets, and piano quintets. 19 artists appeared for the first time and two new ensembles: Divertimenti, and the Viols of the Consort of Musick. Berian Evans, the former viola player of the Alberni Quartet, who had joined another quartet in Australia, was in England for a few months and the opportunity was taken for him to join his "old firm" on January 23rd for performances of Mozart and Brahms two viola quintets. The Committee were relieved not to be liable for his fare.

A very great loss to the Concerts was the death on October 13th of Colin Barralet. Barralets first appear on the Concert Committee in 1894; Colin himself joined the Committee in 1931 and stayed on it for 51 years, working "with the warm and friendly cooperation in a common cause that characterises the Concert Committee to this day" to quote the Annual Report.

The Annual Report of the London Orchestral Concert Board stated: "A word of special gratitude should go to the . . . South Place Sunday Concerts, which must have introduced more great Chamber Music to London audiences than any other concert-giving society."

Dvořák's chamber music, the Britten and Tippett string quartets, and string sextets and quintets generally were characteristic of the 1983/84 season. Twenty artists appeared for the first time, among them two new string quartets: the Fairfield: Ruth Ehrlich, Jennifer Godson, Catherine Marwood, Julia Desbruslais; and the Salomon: Simon Standage, Michaela Comberti, Trevor Jones, Jennifer Ward-Clarke. We welcomed back the Edinburgh String Quartet (with exactly the same players) who had not played for us since the 1977/78 season. This was made possible by the sponsorship of the Standard Life Assurance Company.

The Director of Libraries and Arts of the London Borough of Camden commented: "It (i.e. South Place Concerts) is without doubt the most impressive series of Chamber Music Concerts in London, if not in the entire country."

Sadly recent seasons have seen the deaths of many Concert Committee members all of long service. This time the loss was indeed great to the Committee, to the Concerts as a whole and in particular to our Secretary, George Hutchinson. His wife, Joan, died on July 11th. She had been a very active assistant secretary for 37 years and was loved by all who knew her.

Bartók, Beethoven and Mozart string quartets were featured in the 1984/85 season. We had no difficulty in placing the six Bartók (not the case 27 years ago when we were the first concert organization in London to feature them all in one season), nor the Mozart, but surprisingly there were some gaps in the Beethoven cycle.

The Dartington Ensemble, who played among other things Schubert's "Trout" Quintet, was a new grouping of players well known to our platform. Ten artists appeared for the first time at our Concerts, including one new string quartet team, the Roth: Duncan Riddell, Paul Robson, Elizabeth Turnbull, Stephen Donovan; and another string quartet with an old name but new players: the English: Diana Cummings, Colin Callow, Luciano Iorio, Geoffrey Thomas.

Brahms and Mendelssohn were featured in the 1985/86 season. Thirteen string quartets played for us, one of them new - the Auriol (Robert Bilson, Nicholas Whiting, Brian Schiele and James Halsey). In all there were eighteen newcomers, including "Divertimenti" who played an unusual programme - a Dvořák Sextet, Lutoslowski's Silesian Melodies for four violins, quartets by Frank Bridge and culminating in the Mendelssohn Octet, mandatory if Mendelssohn is featured, but always a delight.

1986-87 - Our 96th Season. Twenty-six Concerts from October to April. The intention is to play all the Beethoven, the ten most famous Mozart and the six Bartók String Quartets. The nineteenth Concert of the season will be our Centenary Celebration on 22nd February, as near as we could get to our first concert in 1887 on 20th February, and will be given in aid of the Musicians' Benevolent Fund. The Lindsay String Quartet will play Beethoven Op. 95 in F, Dvořák American and the Schubert Two Cello Quintet with Douglas Cummings, a typical South Place Programme. With some regret Conway Hall is not being used, since it was felt that the capacity of the Queen Elizabeth Hall was needed to accommodate the larger audience anticipated.

We look back with gratitude to the inspiration and devotion of Alfred J. Clements, to the loyalty of numerous hard-working Committee members, many of whom have spent a lifetime in the service of the Concerts, and to the generous co-operation of musicians whose artistry has created the reputation of the Concerts. We can also be proud of the contribution made to the musical life of the nation, and of the many artists who have made their first or early appearances at our Concerts and have subsequently become famous.

The Centenary Concert is of course just a milestone in the history of the Concerts and there is no reason why they should not go on.

Often when a Concert series depends entirely on voluntary help and more particularly on the driving force of one particular person the withdrawal of that person from the scene means the collapse and end of the series. That did not happen with Clements, for there was someone that shared many of his qualities able to take over. Our present secretary, George who, for 58 years Concert Committee member, 16 years assistant secretary and finally organiser and secretary for the last forty years has brought the Concerts to where they stand today. But the Concerts will continue for many years yet, for although George, who at 81 feels it is time to make way for a younger man, has decided to retire at the end of this season, he is to be followed by Lionel Elton, keen, dedicated, in love with the Concerts. We wish him well.

THE ENSEMBLES

The following articles about most of the ensembles that in more recent years have played a substantial part in maintaining the reputation of the Concerts have been written either by a member of the team - which accounts for their modest tone - or by someone who knows the team well. Lovers of chamber music will know how to redress the balance from their own knowledge of these famous musicians. We feel the varied approach makes for interesting reading and no attempt has been made towards uniformity.

THE AEOLIAN STRING QUARTET

SYDNEY HUMPHREYS, RAYMOND KEENLYSIDE, MARGARET MAJOR, DEREK SIMPSON

FIFTY-EIGHT appearances from 1945 to 1969

In 1927 George Stratton formed the Stratton String Quartet,* a group so successful as to be chosen by Elgar to record his Quartet and Piano Quintet in 1932. During the 1939-45 war Stratton left the Quartet and the name Aeolian was adopted, John Moore, cellist and Watson Forbes, viola, remained, but towards 1969 the Quartet reformed with Sydney Humphreys, Raymond Keenlyside, Margaret Major and Derek Simpson. The Quartet established an international reputation with a full-time programme of concert-giving, broadcasting and recording.

---

*The Stratton String Quartet played 25 times at South Place from 1927 to 1939.

THE ALBERNI STRING QUARTET

HOWARD DAVIS, PETER POPLE, ROGER BEST, DAVID SMITH

FORTY-NINE appearances from 1964-1986

The Alberni String Quartet was formed by four students at the Royal Academy of Music in 1961 and in 1963 became resident quartet to the New Town of Harlow in Essex, a connection they still retain. This appointment, a unique example of civic patronage for chamber music, left the quartet free to travel widely and to develop its career in many ways. In the sixties they were associated with Benjamin Britten, being coached by him in his quartets, and also undertook a residency at Canterbury University in New Zealand for a season; in the seventies they were visiting artists in residence to The University of Western Australia, whilst their American début in New York in 1979 was greeted by the New York Times as "one of the most significant débuts of recent times". They have since toured North America, The Caribbean and South America regularly.

The quartet is well known also for its concerts and workshops for children and, in particular, its courses for quartets at Cambridge University. They have made many highly acclaimed gramophone records which have won various awards including a Grammy nomination for their recording of the Schubert 'cello quintet with the late Thomas Igloi. They are visiting artists in residence to the Royal Scottish Academy for Music and Drama.

The Alberni first appeared at Conway Hall in 1963 and have given concerts in every season since.

THE ALLEGRI STRING QUARTET

KEITH LOVELL, DAVID ROTH, BRUNO SCHRECKER, PETER CARTER

FIFTY-TWO appearances from 1954 to 1987

The Allegri String Quartet has been recognised as among the world's finest for more than thirty years. Since 1954 they have performed regularly in the world's capitals to consistent public and critical acclaim. A measure of their standing was the selection as first choice by the BBC critics in their programme 'Building a Library' of the Allegri's recent recordings of both the Schubert Quartet in D minor ('Death and the Maiden') and the Quintet in C major for two cellos.

1985 has taken them to Europe and North America with appearances at several international festivals, while at home a concentration on the Second Viennese School has led to broadcast performances of Schönberg's Quartets and an appearance in Christopher Nupen's television film on Schönberg and Wittgenstein.

A special feature of the Quartet's work is its association under the auspices of the Radcliffe Trust with the universities of Oxford, Leeds, Hull, Southampton, Bristol and Nottingham, and Dartington College of Arts, which it visits regularly to give concerts and masterclasses. This affords a unique opportunity to explore the lesser known string quartet repertoire under the guidance of the country's most respected academics, and a chance for performer and academic to come together to shed new light on the great classical masterpieces.

THE AMADEUS QUARTET

NORBERT BRAININ, SIGMUND NISSEL, PETER SCHIDLOF, MARTIN LOVETT

ELEVEN appearances from 1947 to 1969

This season the Amadeus Quartet have been playing together for thirty-eight years without a single change of personnel - a unique record in the history of any string quartet. Norbert Brainin, Sigmund Nissel and Peter Schidlof left Vienna for England in 1938. They met Martin Lovett in London in 1947.

Over the years the Amadeus Quartet has received worldwide recognition of their talent. They were awarded the OBE for their services to music by Her Majesty the Queen, Honorary Doctorates from the universities of London and York, the Grosse Verdienstkreuz (Grand Cross of Merit) by the German

Federal Republic and the Ehrenkreuz für Kunst und Wissenschaft (Cross of Honour for Arts and Science) by the Austrian government. Deutsche Grammophon has also presented them with one of the highest awards in the recording world, the "Golden Gramophone", to mark their long association with the company, and a book written by Daniel Snowman called "The Amadeus Quartet - the Men and the Music" has been published by Robson Books.

In September 1986 they took up professorships at the Royal Academy of Music in London with special responsibility for the teaching and performance of chamber music.

THE AMICI STRING QUARTET

NICHOLAS DOWDING, BERNARD RICHARDS, ROBERT HOPE SIMPSON, LIONEL BENTLEY

SIXTY-FOUR appearances from 1956 to 1985

The title "Amici" may suggest a degree of optimism, bearing in mind that such a medium *can* occasionally produce a rather strained atmosphere.

1986 marked the thirtieth anniversary of the first concert performance of the Amici Quartet and is particularly interesting to me because George Hutchinson organised it when we were both coaching string sections of the London School Orchestra.

Our first Conway Hall concert was given the following season and the Quartet has been happily associated with the South Place Sunday Concerts until our last performance there in 1985.

There were changes of personnel over the years and a much regretted break of a year or so while the Quartet reformed, but past and present members remain excellent 'Amici'.

The Quartet has toured throughout the country, in Ireland and on the Continent, broadcast frequently, appeared on Television, performed in the Edinburgh Festival and made a number of recordings.

We have always regarded Conway Hall appearances as Special Occasions.

LIONEL BENTLEY

You must read this book to realise the enormous debt the Concerts owe to the Amici and particularly its leader Lionel Bentley. He backed our obsession with Bartók, and scored a number of firsts in London, helping us to prove that there was an audience for these marvellous six quartets. He first played for us in 1935.

G.H.

THE BLECH STRING QUARTET

KEITH CUMMINGS, LIONEL BENTLEY, HARRY BLECH, DOUGLAS CAMERON

TWENTY-FOUR appearances from 1934 to 1950

They made their important appearance on 6th December 1934 at the Grotrian Hall with a programme that included the last Beethoven and a first performance in England of the Pizzetti Quartet. Very favourable press reviews brought many engagements and Harry Blech eventually left the B.B.C. Symphony Orchestra to concentrate on Chamber Music, here and on the continent, broadcasting and recording.

The war brought changes and the combination shown in the photograph continued very successfully up to 1950 when the London Mozart Players made demands on the conductor Harry Blech which made it necessary for him to choose between the two careers.

THE BOCHMANN QUARTET

MICHAEL BOCHMANN, DAVID ANGEL, MARTIN OUTRAM,
MICHAEL KAZNOWSKI

SEVENTEEN appearances from 1978 to 1987

The Bochman Quartet was formed in 1976 under the guidance of Sidney Griller at the Royal Academy of Music. During its ten years the quartet has seen changes of personnel: the first 'cellist was Sebastian Comberti and the two previous viola players were Garfield Jackson and Gustav Clarkson. The present members have been together since 1983.

They have played throughout the British Isles and much of Europe, appearing at many of the major Festivals and performing frequently at the South Bank concert halls.

They are regularly to be heard on the radio, and have recorded for television both in Britain and abroad.

Since 1983 the quartet has acted as quartet in residence at Southampton University, giving concerts, teaching and coaching.

Recently their recording of Dvořák's opus 96 and opus 34 quartets was released on the N.B.H. label. Future engagements include a Purcell Room series featuring piano quintets, and a tour of the United States.

THE BROSA STRING QUARTET

ANTHONY PINI, DAVID WISE, LEONARD RUBENS, ANTONIO BROSA

SIXTEEN appearances from 1926 to 1938

The Brosa String Quartet was formed in London early in 1925. Their first public appearance in November, 1926 was at a series of recitals at the Grotrian Steinway Hall where they were received with great enthusiasm by public and press. Cyril Scott spoke of "performance beyond all criticism". *The Times* used the word "masterly". *The Manchester Guardian* noted "their quite unusual precision of team work and purity of tone", and the *Morning Post* had "never heard a more satisfactory performance".

"The name of the Brosa String Quartet is one to be remembered", said *Le Figaro. Allgemeine Musikzeitung* was impressed by the "magnificent ensemble" and "marvellous virtuosity".

Brosa had played at the South Place Sunday Concerts in Moorgate, but his now famous quartet made a most generous gesture in giving in 1929 a series of recitals in aid of the building fund of the Conway Hall. At these concerts they were joined by Harriet Cohen, Mark Hambourg and Solomon.

THE CHILINGIRIAN STRING QUARTET

LEVON CHILINGIRIAN PHILIP DE GROOTE

MARK BUTLER CSABA ERDÉLYI

SIXTEEN appearances from 1972 to 1987

The original members of our quartet had all been students at the Royal College of Music during the late sixties, a time when there was a lot of enthusiastic music-making amongst the students themselves. Once spoilt by the challenge of chamber-music, it was no difficult task for Levon to persuade Simon Rowland-Jomes, viola, Philip De Groote, cello and myself to join with him and make quartet-playing our career. Thus, in 1971 we started working together, and shortly after were appointed Resident quartet at the University of Liverpool. In 1976 we had the good fortune to win the Young Concert Artists competition in New York, since when the USA has become the venue for much of our work. Heavy touring commitments took their toll, however, and Simon left the quartet so that he could devote more time to composition, a task sadly impossible to combine with the itinerary of a modern touring string-quartet. Luck came our way, though, when Csaba Erdélyi (a Hungarian) joined us as violist, and we now continued our travels, spending part of each season in the USA, and when at home coach young ensembles at our course at West Dean, Sussex and at the Gardner Arts Centre at the University of Sussex. Forays into Europe, Australia, New Zealand and the Far East complete what has become a busy and stimulating quartet life.

MARK BUTLER

THE COULL STRING QUARTET

ROGER COULL, PHILIP GALLAWAY, JOHN TODD, DAVID CURTIS

FIFTEEN appearances from 1978 to 1986

The Coull String Quartet was formed in 1974 by four students at the Royal Academy of Music under the guidance of Sidney Griller. London débuts in 1977 in the Wigmore Hall and Purcell Room gained critical acclaim, and this was also the year in which they were chosen by Warwick University to become its 'quartet-in-residence' to succeed the Fitzwilliam.

At the time of writing, the quartet has performed throughout the United Kingdom (with an annual tour of the Channel Islands), in most European countries, India, Australia, Malaysia, Hong Kong, the Philippines, and will shortly be undertaking a tour of the USA.

They broadcast regularly for the BBC, by whom they were chosen as its sole representative for the European Broadcasting Union's 'Festival Days' for string quartets in 1983.

The Coull has enjoyed an association with the eminent British composer, Dr. Robert Simpson, and was delighted to have the opportunity of performing his tenth quartet ('For Peace') at South Place (commissioned by them for their tenth anniversary with funds made available by West Midlands Arts Association). They have recorded the tenth and eleventh quartets for Hyperion Records.

The Coull has had only one change of player: John Todd became its cellist in 1985, taking over from Martin Thomas.

THE DELME QUARTET

TEN appearances from 1971 to 1986

The Delmé was founded in 1962 by Granville Delmé Jones, Jurgen Hess, John Underwood and Joy Hall. It gained immediate prominence and was invited to all major Festivals in Europe including Edinburgh and Salzburg. They are particularly well known in Germany and Austria for their Haydn and Beethoven interpretations. They were the first Quartet in Residence at the then new University of Sussex in 1964.

In 1982 five leading composers were commissioned to write works with a definite Haydn connection to celebrate the 250th anniversary of the birth of Haydn and their own 20th anniversary. Five fine works were produced by John McCabe, Christopher Headington, Wilfred Josephs, Daniel Jones and Robert Simpson and they were warmly received at the Wigmore Hall, London.

The Quartet has been led for many years by Galina Solodchin with John Trusler, the bass side of the Quartet being John Underwood viola and Robert Bailey cello.

JEREMY WILLIAMS, GALINA SOLODCHIN, JOHN UNDERWOOD, ROBERT BAILEY

THE EDINBURGH QUARTET

MILES BASTER, MICHAEL BEESTON, PETER MARKHAM, MARK BAILEY

SIXTEEN appearances from 1963 to 1986

The Edinburgh Quartet is Scotland's foremost chamber ensemble. Its foundation was the inspiration of the late Sydney Newman, professor of music at Edinburgh University, who succeeded in estáblishing at Edinburgh Britain's first university-based string quartet.

In addition to its regular concerts at Edinburgh's Reid and Queen's Hall, Hopetoun House, etc., the Quartet undertakes regular tours to all parts of Scotland and frequent visits to other parts of the UK. After their success at the Evian les Bains International Quartet Competition foreign tours have become increasingly prestigious, with recent Canadian and USSR tours being followed by visits to the Middle East, Spain and the USA. Having played in almost all European countries, links between East and West have been an invaluable part of the Quartet's growth.

A keen interest in music education has led to them working as Quartet in Residence at the Aberdeen International Youth Festival for several years. In addition, they regularly coach the students of the Royal Scottish Academy of Music and Drama in chamber music.

With regular broadcasting on BBC radio and nine TV appearances this season alone, The Edinburgh Quartet looks set to enter its most exciting period yet.

THE FITZWILLIAM STRING QUARTET

IOAN DAVIES, JONATHAN SPAREY, DANIEL VISMAN, ALAN GEORGE

FIFTEEN appearances from 1973 to 1985

Hailed as possibly the most exciting young string quartet to have emerged within the last ten years, the Fitzwilliam String Quartet rapidly established a reputation at the highest international level.

Early in their professional life they became Quartet in Residence at the University of York and indeed throughout most of their career the Quartet maintained a close association with that University.

One important aspect of the Quartet's early career was their close association with the music of Dmitri Shostakovich. They gave the British and American premières of his last three string quartets and when they performed the complete cycle of his quartets in New York, *Time Magazine* called it 'the instrumental highlight of the New York Season'. It is therefore highly appropriate that they joined the Borodin String Quartet in a performance of the Shostakovitch Octet in the Queen Elizabeth Hall in February 1986 in the opening concert of the Borodin's own cycle of the Shostakovich Quartets.

The Fitzwilliam Quartet recorded exclusively for Decca and their recordings won numerous awards, including the Grand Prix du Disque (France), two nominations for the American Grammy award and the Gramophone award for the best chamber music record of the year 1978. Due for release is their recent recording of Shostakovich's Piano Quintet with Ashkenazy.

A highly successful appearance at the 1985 Edinburgh Festival heralded a busy season for the Fitzwilliam Quartet. They were in great demand internationally and in the following season gave concerts in Japan, the United States, Sweden, Switzerland, Finland, Holland and Belgium.

THE GRILLER STRING QUARTET

PHILIP BURTON, JACK O'BRIEN, SIDNEY GRILLER, COLIN HAMPTON

THIRTY-FOUR appearances from 1929 to 1946

In 1926 Sidney Griller, Jack O'Brien, Philip Burton and Colin Hampton played together as students at the Royal Academy and were coached by Lionel Tertis. As their friendship and their interest in string quartet playing grew, they resolved to make chamber music playing their life's work! To make it easier for them to have the necessary many hours of ensemble practice, they shared a large old house which was big enough also for them to be able to stay together even when marriage put pressure on accommodation.

In 1928 there were few engagements for young quartets, but Mr. Clements recognised young genius when he heard it and soon they were regular players at South Place Concerts. This frequent platform brought them wide recognition, and in the years leading up to 1939 they were recognised as being unsurpassed as interpreters of the whole range of string quartets.

After the war, they made another appearance at Conway Hall, but very soon they went to the University of California, Berkeley. This was not isolation. Their tours and recordings kept the whole musical world in touch. But sadly in 1961 the quartet was disbanded on the death of Philip Burton, the viola player.

Throughout the whole of the Quartet's existence the personnel never changed.

THE HIRSCH STRING QUARTET

LEONARD HIRSCH, LEONARD DIGHT, STEPHEN SHINGLES
FRANCISCO GABARRO

FIFTY-EIGHT appearances from 1938 to 1960

The Hirsch String Quartet made their first public appearance in 1928. The players were Leonard Hirsch, Reginald Stead, Maurice Ward and Haydn Rogerson. The young team rapidly established a reputation for fine performances so that by 1934

The Times was speaking of "ensemble playing of high quality" and the London correspondent of *The Manchester Guardian* saying of them that they were "one of the best chamber music teams permanently resident in the country - if not the best".

Over the years the busy life of recitals, broadcasts, engagements up and down the country at music clubs and continental tours paid tribute to their reputation as an outstanding ensemble, and it was a great loss to the musical world when in 1960 the Quartet finally disbanded.

Over such a stretch of time, 32 years, it was inevitable that there would be changes of personnel, but the ability of the leader to find sympathetic partners matched his qualities as an outstanding interpretative artist, so that the Quartet maintained its excellence throughout.

The photograph shows the Hirsch String Quartet as it was in later years.

THE LINDSAY STRING QUARTET

PETER CROPPER, RONALD BIRKS, ROBIN IRELAND, BERNARD GREGOR-SMITH

TWENTY appearances from 1971 to 1987

The Lindsay Quartet is securely established in the forefront of Britain's chamber ensembles. They tour the world extensively as well as appearing regularly at leading festivals in this country, such as Edinburgh, Bath, Cheltenham, Aldeburgh and the Proms.

They record for ASV and have completed the complete cycles of the Bartók and Beethoven Quartets. In 1984 the Quartet received the Gramophone Chamber Award for the box set of the late Beethoven Quartets and their complete Beethoven is increasingly being regarded by critics as the definitive version of these works, which could be said to represent the core of the quartet repertoire. The recently released recording of Schubert's String Quintet is the first in a project cycle of Schubert recordings.

A busy international schedule included in the autumn of 1985 their third nationwide tour of the USA when they played at Washington's prestigious library of Congress which, said the *Washington Post*, "mixed a combination of musical purity and audacity to perfection". 1985/6 also included Paris, Zurich, Warsaw, Frankfurt, Hanover, Salzburg, Stockholm and Dublin. In 1987 a further extensive tour of Italy is planned.

The Quartet is in residence at the University of Manchester, where as well as giving regular concert seasons, it directs seminars on the quartet repertoire, coaches chamber ensembles and provides individual instrumental tuition.

ROBERT MASTERS PIANO QUARTET

ROBERT MASTERS, NANNIE JAMIESON, MURIEL TAYLOR, KINLOCH ANDERSON

SIXTEEN appearances from 1947 to 1963

The Quartet was formed at Dartington Hall in 1939. They rapidly acquired a world-wide reputation, making many tours, exploited fully a classical and modern repertoire of string and piano trios and piano quartets. For eleven years they ran a very successful summer school in Berkshire.

There was only one change of personnel over the lifetime of the ensemble. Kinloch Anderson eventually became chief recording manager of HMV and his place was taken by Ross Pratt.

From 1958 Robert Masters became leader of the Bath Festival Orchestra later called the Menuhin Orchestra, and in 1961 he led the London Mozart Players. Increasing activities of both these groups, containing the Quartet's three string players, as well as their teaching commitments made the Quartet's continuance difficult and they gave their last concert together in 1963. Robert Master's association with Yehudi Menuhin in Chamber Music concerts and recordings continued.

Ross Pratt returned to Canada to a teaching post in Quebec.

THE LONDON FESTIVAL PLAYERS

FREDERICK RIDDLE NORMAN JONES
MARY MURDOCH MARY RYAN TREVOR WILLIAMS

SIXTEEN appearances from 1971 to 1986

Although now it is quite independent, hence the present name, the London Festival Players were earlier the Tilford Festival Ensemble, for it came out of the Tilford Bach Society which with kindred activities still flourishes under the direction of Denys Darlow. The usual combination is flute, oboe, violin, cello and harpsichord. Three of the founder members, Mary Ryan, flute, Mary Murdoch, oboe and Derek Stevens, harpsichord are still together, along with Trevor Williams, violin, who joined them in 1967. Cellists have included Olga Hegedus and Ross Pople but Norman Jones has played with them now for several years. Violists have included Christopher Wellington and Frederick Riddle. Daphne Ibbott plays the piano.

Their repertoire is very varied but in particular includes Trevor Williams' and Mary Ryan's arrangement of Bach's Art of Fugue and the Musical Offering and in addition to music of the eighteenth and nineteenth centuries, such works as Schönberg's Pierrot Lunaire and Kammersymphonie arranged by Webern.

The London Festival Players have maintained a close connection with the South Place Concerts over many years.

THE MELOS ENSEMBLE

RICHARD ADENEY, Fl., PETER GRAEME, Ob., GERVASE DE PEYER, Cl., WILLIAM WATERHOUSE, Bn., NEILL SANDERS, Hn., EMANUEL HURWITZ, Vn., CECIL ARONOWITZ, Va., TERENCE WEIL, Vc., ADRIAN BEERS, DB., LAMAR CROWSON, Pf.

FOURTEEN appearances from 1953 to 1969

This famous ensemble brought fine players together for the exceptional and larger chamber music groupings, and continues to do so.

THE PARIKIAN-MILNE-FLEMING TRIO

MANOUG PARIKIAN, HAMISH MILNE, AMARYLLIS FLEMING

SEVEN appearances from 1978 to 1985*

In 1976 three distinguished soloists - Manoug Parikian, Amaryllis Fleming and Bernard Roberts - were invited by the Arts Council to combine their talents in a concert to celebrate the 75th anniversary of the Wigmore Hall. The venture was so successful that the artists formed a permanent ensemble which became a highly esteemed feature of the musical scene, broadcasting regularly and appearing at major festivals and concert societies to the highest acclaim from the critics who pronounced them "a piano trio rivalled by few in the world today" (*The Guardian*). In September 1984 the trio reformed with the

*Although the members had played many times before, here is recorded their appearances as a trio.

pianist Hamish Milne as the Parikian-Milne-Fleming Trio, increasing its already extensive repertoire.

The compelling and dynamic interpretations of the ensemble and their unique warmth, clarity and fusion of sound make the trio one of the most exciting chamber ensembles before the public today.

ALEXANDER YOUNG (tenor) — REX STEPHENS (piano)

1954-1969

IAN PARTRIDGE (tenor) — JENNIFER PARTRIDGE (piano)

1970 onwards

Speak of a famous lieder singer and straightway his partner comes to mind.

THE MUSICIANS' BENEVOLENT FUND

The Musicians' Benevolent Fund was founded in 1921 in memory of Gervase Elwes by his friends who wished to commemorate in a practical way the help he gave to the less fortunate members of his profession. One of the features of the support enjoyed by the Fund since that date has been the unstinting help given by professional musicians, and an outstanding example of this is the concert organized annually by the South Place Sunday Concerts. Since 1924 the speakers and artists who have given their services have been:

1924 Harry Plunket Greene. Wood Smith Quartet, Ethel Attwood, Ethel Hobday, Jeffrey Booth, John Goss, E.J. Moeran, Roger Quilter.

1925 Lady Maud Warrender. Grimson Quartet, Evelyn Amherst, Ethel Hobday, Arthur Cranmer.

1926 Victor Beigel. Spencer Dyke Quartet, Harry Plunket Greene, Samuel Liddle, Evelyn Stuart.

1927 Sir John Goss. Kutcher Quartet, Lily Henkel, Dilys Jones, Berkeley Mason.

1928 Mrs. Robert Henderson. Stratton Quartet, Ella Ivimey, Dorothea Webb, Rae Robertson.

1929 Franklyn Kelsey. Bessie Rawlins Quartet, Carda Kelsey, Franklyn Kelsey, Lloyd Powell.

1930 Spencer Dyke Quartet, Ella Ivimey, Tatiana Makushina, Reginald Paul.

1931 Mrs. Robert Henderson. Entente Quartet, Ethel Hobday, Harry Plunket Greene, Samuel Liddle.

1932 Lady Maud Warrender. Rowena Franklin Quartet, Edith Ashby, Gilbert Bailey.

1933 Mrs. Robert Henderson. Bessie Rawlins Quartet, Bertram Ayrton, Gerald Moore.

1934 Harry Plunket Greene. Griller Quartet, Charles Draper, Samuel Liddle.

1935 Mrs. Laura Henderson. New English Quartet, Ethel Attwood, Arthur Cranmer, Maurice Cole.

1936 Harry Plunket Greene. Whinyates Quartet, Clive Carey, Ella Ivimey, Richard H. Walthew.

1937 Reginald Paul Piano Quartet, Mary Macnally, Gertrude Seymour.
1938 Frank Howes. Reginald Paul Quartet, Dorothy D'Orsay, Cecilia Trimby.
1939 Sybil Eaton. Brosa Quartet, Lance Dossor.
1948 Edric Cundell. Aeolian Quartet, Lance Dossor.
1949 Hubert Foss. Harry Isaacs Piano Trio.
1950 Marion Scott. Hirsch Quartet, Harry Isaacs.
1951 Herbert Fryer. New London Quartet.
1952 Dr. Greenhouse-Allt. Aleph Quartet, Kenneth Essex.
1953 Harold Craxton. Peter Gibbs Quartet.
1954 Dr. Herbert Howells. Ethel Bartlett, Rae Robertson.
1955 Sir Reginal Thatcher. Martin Quartet, Wilfrid Parry.
1956 Sir Steuart Wilson. Aeolian Quartet.
1957 Bernard Shore. Allegri Quartet, Terence Weil.
1958 Stuart Robertson. Amici Quartet, Thea King.
1959 Ivor James, CBE. London Quartet, Eric Harrison.
1960 George Baker. Quartet Pro Musica, Celia Arieli.
1961 Parry Jones. Dumka Piano Trio.
1962 Mrs. Ralph Vaughan Williams. Martin Quartet, Wilfrid Parry.
1963 Robert Easton. Robert Masters Piano Quartet, J. Edward Merrett.
1964 David Martin. Aeolian Quartet.
1965 Wilfrid Parry. Amici Quartet.
1966 Rev. Canon R. Tydeman. Dartington Quartet.
1967 George Hutchinson. London Quartet.
1968 Joan Davies. English Quartet, Thea King.
1969 Amadeus Quartet, Gervase de Peyer.
1970 Wilfrid Parry. Alberni String Quartet.
1971 Max Gilbert. Gabrieli String Quartet.
1972 Lady Barbirolli. Georgian String Quartet, James Walker.
1973 Dame Eva Turner. Dartington String Quartet.
1974 Sir Thomas Armstrong. Gabrieli String Quartet.
1975 Alvar Lidell. Haffner String Quartet.
1976 Gerald MacDonald. Linsay String Quartet.
1977 Mrs. Ralph Vaughan Williams. Chilingirian String Quartet.
1978 Julian Lloyd Webber. Fitzwilliam String Quartet.

1979 Philip Cranmer. Medici String Quartet.
1980 Felicity Lott. Allegri String Quartet.
1981 Ian Wallace. Alberni String Quartet, Moray Welsh.
1982 Lady Barbirolli. Amici String Quartet.
1983 Sir Anthony Lewis. Lindsay String Quartet, Imogen Cooper.
1984 Martin Williams. Chilingirian String Quartet.
1985 Michael Gough Matthews. Fitzwilliam String Quartet.
1986 Dr. Jane Glover. Allegri String Quartet, Patrick Ireland.
1987 Lindsay String Quartet, Douglas Cummings.

CLEMENTS MEMORIAL PRIZE

The Clements Memorial Prize was inaugurated in 1939 from funds resulting from a public appeal which were later supplemented by legacies of £800 from Mr. Peters, a personal friend of the Clements and £500 from Mrs. Clements. It consists of a money prize for a chamber music work awarded biennially. In 1986 the prize was £500. Full particulars can be obtained from the Honorary Secretary, Clements Memorial Prize, Conway Hall, Red Lion Square, London WClR 4RL, enclosing a stamped addressed envelope. Prize-winners since 1939: Frederick T. Durrant, William Wordsworth, Bernard Stevens, A. Hawthorne Baker, David Wynne, David Gow, Malcolm Macdonald, P. Raciine Fricker, Jean Coulthard and Doreen Carwithen, Peter Hodgson, Iain Hamilton, Hugo Cole, Reginald Smith Brindle, Raymond Hockley, Geoffrey Winters, Michael Rose, Ian Spooner, Alan Ridout, Jonathan Harvey, Sebastian Forbes, Trevor Hold, Justin Connolly, Geoffrey Poole, Patric Standford, David Niven, Christopher Bochmann, Ian McQueen, Michael Philpot, Richard Steinitz, Martin Davies, James Clarke, Robin Walker.

MUSIC PERFORMED

with the number of times each Work has been given

NONETS

Gounod (Fl 2Ob 2Cl 2Bn 2H) 1
Rheinberger Efl Op139 1
Spohr F Op31 2

OCTETS

Beethoven Efl Op103 1
Cameron, John Cl Bn H St Qt Db In Celebration 1
Cole, Hugo (Wind) 1
Ferguson, Howard 2
Gade F Op17 3
Glière D Op5 1
Malling, O. Dmi Op50 1
Mendelssohn Efl Op20 21
Mozart Serenade Efl K375 (wind) 1
Cmi K388 2
Raff C Op176 Double St Qt 1
Schubert F D803 23
Shostakovich (two pieces) Dble St Qt Op11 1
Spohr Dble St Qt
Dmi Op65 4
Efl Op77 1
Emi Op87 6
Gmi Op136 2
Svendsen A Op3 12

SEPTETS

Bach Art of Fugue 2
Beethoven Efl Op20 15
d'Indy Chanson et Danses 1
Hollander, B. Efl Op28 6
Ravel Introduction and Allegro Gfl, Hp Fl Cl St Qt 5

SEXTETS

Bach Musical Offering 2
(Ricercare alone) 3
Beethoven Dfl Op81b 5
Bennett, W.S. Fshmi Op8 1
Berkeley, Lennox Cl Hn St Qt 1
Börressen G Op5 16
Brahms Bfl Op18 18
G Op36 14
Bridge, F. 1
Chausson D Op21 Concerto Pf Vn St Qt 7
Dvořák A Op48 12
Fuhrmeister
(Wind) Op6 No1 1
(Wind) Op6 No2 1
Gade Efl Op44 4
Glière Cmi Op1 6
Bmi Op7 1
Haydn (Echo) 1
Holbrooke, J. Op24 1
Fmi Op33 1
Fmi Op43 1
Op46 2
Jadassohn, G. Op100 2
Janáček 1
Juon, P. Cmi Op22 1
Lawrence, F. 1
Mendelssohn D Op110 1
Mozart Divertimenti
F K247 2
Bfl K287 5
D K334 8
F K522 1
Quef C Op44 1
Rietz Concertstück 1
Schönberg Dmi Op4 (Verklärte Nacht) 8
Spain-Dunk Emi Op55 1
Strauss R. Capriccio Op85 2
Tchaikovsky Dmi Op70 13
Thuille Bfl Op6 4
Weingartner Emi Op33 1

STRING QUINTETS

Beethoven Efl Op4 1
C Op29 12
Boccherini C 2Vn Va2Vc 4
D 2Vn Va 2Vc 1
Brahms F Op88 6
G Op111 20
Dvořák G Op77 St Qt Db 7
Efl Op97 11
Gade Emi Op8 2
Glazounov A Op39 1
Goldmark Ami Op9 2Vn Va 2Vc 2
Haensel, P. No4 F Op28 2
Mendelssohn A Op18 7
Bfl Op87 6
Mozart Bfl K174 1
Cmi K406 11
C K515 15
Gmi K516 28
D K593 10
Efl K614 8
Onslow Cmi Op80 1
Parry Efl 2
Ries Dmi Op68 1

Schubert C D956
2Vn Va 2VC 26
Spohr Op33 No1 1
G Op33 No2 2
Bmi Op69 1
Svendsen C Op5 4
Taneiew G Op14 1
Vaughan-Williams
Phantasy Dmi 4

CLARINET QUINTETS

Bliss 4
Brahms Op115 26
Coleridge-Taylor Fsh mi 6
Durrant Efl 1
Frankel Op28 1
Gow, David 1
Holbrooke, J. G Op27 1
Howells, H. Op31
Rhapsodic 1
Jacob, Gordon 1
Mozart A K581 29
Reger A Op146 1
Somervell, A. G 2
Walthew, R. Efl 4
Weber Bfl Op34 3

PIANO QUINTETS

Arensky D Op51 3
Bax 4
Bloch No1 6
Brahms Fmi Op34 52
Bridge, F. Dmi 6
Buesst, V. 1
Collingwood, L. A 1
De Castillon Efl Op1 1
D'Erlanger Cmi 1
Dohnanyi Cmi Op1 9
Eflmi Op26 7
Dubois, T. 1
Durrant Cmi 1
Dvořák A Op81 63
Elgar Ami Op84 24
Fauré Dmi Op89 1
Forbes, Sebastian 1
Franck Fmi 45
Friskin Cmi Op1 9
Goetz, H. Cmi Op16 5
Goldmark Bfl Op30 9
Harty, H. F Op12 2
Holbrooke, J. Cmi Op49 2
Hummel Efl Op87
Pf Vn Va Vc Db 3
Lauber, J. F Op6 1
Leech, K. Cmi Op7 1
Malling, O. E Op40 2
Novak Ami Op12 2
Prout G Op3 1
Reizenstein D 1
Rheinberger C Op114 6
Rozycki, L. Op35 2
Saint-Saëns Ami Op14 1
Schmitt, F. Bmi Op51 2
Schubert D667 Trout
Pf Vn Va Vc Db 24
Schumann Efl Op44 53
Sgambati Bfl Op5 2
Shostakovich Op57 8
Sinding Emi Op5 11
Speight, J. Efl 1
Spohr Dmi Op130 1
Stanford Dmi Op25 22
Swepstone, E. Emi 4
Taneiew Gmi Op30 2
Torelli Op6 1
Walthew, R. Fmi 8
Phantasy Emi & ma 8
Wolf-Ferrari Dfl Op6 2
Ysaÿe, Théo B. Op5 1

WIND QUINTETS

Barthé 1
Chrétien, H. 1
Fricker, R. 2
Ibert (3 short pieces) 1
Klughart Op39 1
Lefebre, C. Suite 1
Mozart (arr.Baines)K270
Divertimento No14
Bfl 2
Horn Quintet K407 8
Pessard 1
Pierné 1
Rees 1
Villa-Lobos 1

UNCLASSIFIED QUINTETS

Baker, A.H. Ob St Qt 1
Bax Hp St Qt 1
Ob St Qt 1
Beethoven Efl Op16
Pf Ob Cl Bn Hn 7
Bliss Ob St Qt 1
Debussy Danse Sacrée
et Danse Profane Hp
St Qt 2
Fogg,E. Fl Ob Cl Bn Pf 1
Mozart Efl K452
Pf Ob Cl Bn Hn 9
Rimsky-Korsakov Bfl
OpPosth Pf Fl Cl Bn
Hn 1
Roussel Serenade Op30
Fl Vn Va Vc Hp 1
Swepstone, E. D Hn
St Qt 1
Efl Pf Wind 1
Walker, E. Bmi Hn St Qt 5

STRING QUARTETS

Arensky Ami Op35a 2Vc 4
Arriaga No1 Dmi 4
No2 A 3
No3 2
No5 1

Work	No.
Bach Art of Fugue	
Transc. Watson	
Forbes 2Vc	4
Bartók No1 Ami Op7	9
No2 Ami Op17	14
No3 Csh	10
No4 C	9
No5 Bfl	10
No6 D	15
Bax G	9
F	1
Beethoven	
F Op18 No1	26
F Op18 No2	27
D Op18 No3	26
Cmi Op18 No4	38
A Op18 No5	19
Bfl Op18 No6	17
F Op59 No1	35
Emi Op59 No2	33
C Op59 No3	40
Efl Op74	34
Fmi Op95	48
Efl Op127	28
Bfl Op130	24
Csh mi Op131	17
Ami Op132	23
Bfl Op130 with	
Op133	5
Bfl Op133 Grosse	
Fuge	6
F Op135	32
Blanc, A. F Op38	1
Bliss, A. No1	4
No2 Fmi	2
Bloch No1 Bmi	3
No2	4
No3	2
No4	2
No5	1
In the Mountains	2
Night	2
Prelude	2
Three Landscapes	2
Boccherini A Op6 No6	1
Op24 No5	1
Gmi Op27 No2	1
Bonavia Emi	1
Borodin A No1	6
D No2	10
Bowen, Y. G Op46	1
Bowman, A.	1
Boyce Suite	1
Boyes, D. Emi	1
Brahms Cmi Op51 No1	33
Ami Op51 No2	34
Bfl Op67	18
Bree, van No3 Dmi	1
Bridge, F. Emi	2
Fma and mi	1
Gmi	1
Cherry Ripe	2
Sally in our Alley	2
Sir Roger de Coverley	1
Three Idylls	6
Three Noveletten	2
Britten No1 D Op25	6
No2 C Op36	4
No3 Op94	2
Bush Dialectic	2
Carwithen, D No1	1
Cherubini No2 C	2
No3 Dmi	1
Cole, H.	1
Coleridge-Taylor Op5	1
Cundell, E. No4 C Op27	1
Coulthard	1
Davies, Walford	
Peter Pan	2
Davies, J.D. Variations	
Londonderry Air	1
Debussy Gmi Op10	34
Delius	2
Dittersdorf A	1
Efl	12
Dohnanyi A Op7	5
Dfl Op15	17
Ami Op33	3
Dvořák Fmi	1
Ami Op16	4
Dmi Op34	7
Efl Op51	27
C Op61	7
E Op80	8
F Op96	33
Afl Op105	8
G Op106	15
Elgar Op83	11
Farjeon, H. Bfl	1
Fauré Op121	1
Franck D	8
Frankel No2 Op15	2
No3	1
Friskin Phantasy D	2
Fuchs, R. C Op71	1
Gardiner, B.	1
Glazounov F Op10	1
Op15	2
Op26	1
Ami Op64	2
Dmi Op70	7
Gadsby, Tony	1
Goossens,E. By the Tarn	3
Jack O'Lantern	3
Grieg Gmi op27	10
Hamilton, Iain	1
Harty, H. A Op5	5
Harvey, Jonathan	1
Haydn Efl Op1 No2	1
E Op3 No1	2
Bfl Op3 No4	3
F Op3 No5	7
A Op3 No6	2
Ami Op9 No1	1
Efl Op9 No2	3
Dmi Op9 No4	2
G Op17 No5	1
Efl Op20 No1	4
C Op20 No2	6
Gmi Op20 No3	2
D Op20 No4	10
Fmi Op20 No5	12
A Op20 No6	3
Bmi Op33 No1	3
Efl Op33 No2	10
C Op33 No3	10
G Op33 No5	1
D Op33 No6	1
Dmi Op42	2

Bfl Op50 No1 6
C Op50 No2 1
F Op50 No5 3
D Op50 No6 6
G Op54 No1 13
C Op54 No2 9
E Op54 No3 6
C Op64 No1 3
B Op64 No2 2
Bfl Op64 No3 4
G Op64 No4 9
D Op64 No5 21
Efl Op64 No6 17
D Op71 No2 4
Efl Op71 No3 1
C Op4 No1 11
F Op4 No2 3
Gmi Op74 No3 15
G Op76 No1 17
Dmi Op76 No2 23
C Op76 No3 21
Bfl Op76 No4 23
D Op76 No5 16
Efl Op76 No6 8
G Op77 No1 32
F Op77 No2 18
Bfl Op103 (Unfinished) 6
Seven Last Words (arr.) 1
Henschel, G. Efl Op55 1
Hindemith Efl No5 1
No6 2
Holbrooke, J. Dmi & ma Op17 2
Two Impressions Op59a 1
Hollander, B. Csh mi Op31 1
Dmi 1
Holst, Imogen Phantasy Qt 1
Howells, H.
Phantasy Qt Op25 2
Lady Audrey Suite 2
Hummel C Op30 No1 1
Hurlstone A ma & mi 1
Janaček No2 (1928)
Intimate Letters 2
Jongen, J.A. Op50 3
Joseph, J. 1
Kässmayer Op14 4
Kodaly No1 Op2 2
No2 Op10 4
Krenek No7 Op96 1
Leighton, Kenneth No2 1
Seven Variations 1
Locke, M. G No6 1
Maconchy No3 Op15 1
Malipiero
Stornelli e Ballate 1
No6 L'arca di Noè 1
Martinu, B. No4 1
Maxwell Davies (1961) 1
McEwen, J.B. Ami 1
Cmi 1
Threnody 1
Biscay 3
Seven Bagatelles 3
Mendelssohn
Efl Op12 No1 10
Ami Op13 5
D Op44 No1 11
Emi Op44 No2 11
Efl Op44 No3 6
Fmi Op80 2
Capriccio Op81 9
Miaskowsky Op33 No2 1
Milhaud, D. No7 (1925) 1
Moeran, E.J. Ami 5
Morris, R.O. Phantasy Qt 1
Mozart D K136 1
G K80 1
F K168 1
Dmi K173 1
G K337 4
G K387 29
Dmi K421 42
Efl K428 30
Bfl K458 45
A K464 17
C K465 47
D K499 25
D K575 28
Bfl K589 19
F K590 15
Divertimento No2
Bfl 1
Mailander Qt No4
K213 1
Serenade K525 (arr.) 1
Murgier, J. Dfl 1
Nielson No3 Efl 1
No4 F Op44 1
Onslow Ami Op4 No3 1
Pijper No1 1
No2 1
No3 1
No4 2
No5 1
Pizzetti A 1
D 3
Prokofiev Op50 2
No2 in F Op92 1
Purcell Fantasia Cmi
No4 1
Chacony 5
Ravel, F. 31
Rawsthorne No2 2
No3 (1965) 1
Theme and Variations 2
Reger Fsh mi Op121 1
Roussel Op45 1
Rubbra No1 Fmi Op35 2
No2 Efl Op73 3
Schönberg No1 Dmi Op7 2
No2 Op10 with soprano 2
No3 Op30 1
No4 Op37 2
Schubert Ami D804 35
Efl D87 6
E D353 2
G D887 12
Bfl D112 3
Dmi D810 35
Gmi D173 3

Cmi D703
(Quartettsatz) 24
Schumann Ami Op41
No1 14
F Op41 No2 4
A Op41 No3 11
Seiber Op1 No1 (1924) 2
Shostakovich No1 C
Op49 5
No2 Op68 4
No3 Op73 4
No4 Op83 4
No5 Bfl Op92 7
No6 4
No7 Fsh mi Op108 5
No8 Op110 7
No9 Op117 2
No10 Op118 3
No11 Op122 1
No12 Op133 1
No13 Op138 1
Sibelius Dmi Op56
Voces Intimae 19
Smetana Emi
Aus meinem Leben 22
Smith, L.D. 1
Smyth, E. Emi 1
Speight, J. Gmi 1
Ariel 1
Cobweb, Moth &
Mustard Seed 1
Puck 1
Queen Mab -
Titania 1
Spohr Gmi Op4 No2 5
C Op29 No2 1
Emi Op45 No2 1
Stanford Ami Op45 4
Dmi Op64 3
Gmi Op99 1
Stevens, B. No2 Op34 1
Theme & Variations 1
Stratton, G. Fmi 1
Phantasy 1
Strauss, R. A Op2 1
Stravinsky Concertino 1
Suk Bfl Op11 1
Meditation on a
Chorale Op35 2
Svendsen Ami Op1 6
Swepstone, E. Lyrical
Cycle 1
Szervanszky C Op37 1
Tailleferre 1
Taylor, Coleridge Op5 1
Tchaikovsky D Op11 16
F Op22 2
Efl mi Op30 3
Telemann Sonata in A 1
Ten Russian Com-
posers Qt 1
Tippett No1 (1935 rev.
1943) 1
No2 Fsh mi 6
Troup Romance 2
Turina La Oración del
Torero 6
Vaughan Williams
No1 Gmi 4
No2 Ami 4
Ami (1945) 1
Verdi Emi Op68 7
Vitali, G.B. Capriccio 1
Volkmann Gmi Op14 2
Emi Op35 1
Walenn, G. Fmi 1
Walsworth, I. (1944) 1
Walthew, R. E 2
Bfl 1
Efl 4
Six Lyrical Pieces 1
Warner, H.W. D Op15
No1 2
F Op15 No2 1
Walton Ami 5
Webern 6 Bagatelles Op9 1
Whitaker, G.
Theme & Variations 1
Williams, Gerard No2 2
Wolf Italian Serenade 16
Wood, C. D 3
F 1
Ami 2
Variations on an
Irish Folk Tune 1
Wood-Smith, R.F.
Miniature Suite 1
Prelude & Scherzo 1
Wood, H. Phantasy 2
Wordsworth, W.
No2 Bfl (1943) 1
No4 Ami Op47 1
D 1
Wyck, van 1
Wynne, David No1
Clements Prize 1944 1

PIANO QUARTETS

Alwyn, W. Rhapsody 1
Ashton, A. Cmi Op90 1
Bach, J.C. G 1
Bax (one movement) 1
Beethoven Efl Op16 14
Bliss Ami Op5 1
Boisdeffre Gmi Op13 1
Brahms Gmi Op25 25
A Op26 24
Cmi Op60 19
Bridge Fantasy 1
Bush Op5 1
Causson A Op30 7
Cobb, G.F.E. Op34 1
Copland 1
Dussek Efl Op56 1
Dvořák D Op23 10
Op47 2Vn Vc Pf 3
Efl Op87 23
Fauré Cmi Op15 17
Gmi Op45 10
Fibich Emi Op11 1
Frankel Op26 1
Fuchs, R. Bmi Op75 1
Goetz, E. Op6 1
Grainger, P. Handel in
the Strand (arr.) 1
Holbrooke Gmi Op21 1
Howells, H. Ami Op21 4

Hurlstone, W.Y. Emi Op43 8
Jongen, J. Efl Op23 7
Kiel Ami Op43 1
Leipold, E. 1
Loeillet Bmi 2
Mackenzie Efl 3
Martinu No1 (1942) 1
Mendelssohn Cmi Op1 2
Fmi Op2 2
Bmi Op3 6
Molique Efl Op71 1
Mozart Gmi K478 25
Ef K493 18
Pope, Peter 1
Rabl Efl Op1 1
Rheinberger Efl Op38 13
Rubinstein C Op66 1
Saint-Saëns Bfl Op41 6
Schlegel, L. C Op14 1
Schmitt Hasards Op96 1
Schubert Adagio and Rondo Concertante 1
Schumann Efl Op47 24
Shedlock, J.S. Ami 1
Speight, J. G 1
Stanford F Op15 1
Stratton, G. C 2
Strauss, R. Cmi Op13 2
Swepstone, E. Ami 2
Turina Ami 1
Walker, E. D 1
Cmi 2
Walthew, R. Gmi 9
Walton Dmi 2
Weber Bfl 2
Wolstenholme E Op87 1

UNCLASSIFIED QUARTETS

Bach, J.S. Ob Vn Vn Vc in C 1
Bach, W.F. Fl Vn Vc Hpcd in D 1
Berkeley Ob Vn Vn Vc 1
F Vn Vc Hpchd 1
Boyce Hpchd Vn Vn Vc 1
Britten Phantasy Ob Qt 1
Cole, Hugo Ob Qt 1
Cooke, Arnold Ob Qt 1
Hodgson Fl Qt 1
Mozart Fl Qt K285 5
Fl Qt K298 2
Ob Qt K370 9
Pergolesi Ob Qt in D arr. Peggy Sampson 1
Purcell Sonata No6 Chaconne Hpchd Vn Va Vc 1
Fl Ob Cl Bn arr. Vinter 1
Schubert Guitar Qt 1
Shield Ob Qt F Op3 No2 1
Rawsthorne Cl Qt 1
Telemann F Vn Ob Cont. Ami 1
Wordsworth, W. Ob Qt Op44 2

STRING TRIOS

Austin Suite No8 1
Bach 3 part invention (arr.) 1
Preludes & Fugues Nos 3 and 4 arr. Mozart 1
Beethoven Efl Op3 2
(Serenade) D Op8 10
G Op9 No1 6
D Op9 No2 3
Dmi Op9 No3 11
Berkeley, Lennox (1943) 3
Dohnanyi C Op10 Serenade 9
Dvořák C Op74 Vn Vn Va 4
Finzi Prelude and Fugue 2
Françaix (1933) 3
Frankel Op3 1
Gibbons 2
Haydn G Op53 No1 3
Bfl Op53 No3 1
Hellmesberger 1
Hilton Six Pieces 1
Hindemith No1 Op34 (1924) 1
No 2 (1933) 2
Hollander Three Pieces 1
Moeran, E.J. G 1
Mozart Prelude & Fugue arr. K404a 3
Divertimento Efl K563 7
Purcell Three Fantasies 1
3 Two part Fantasies arr. Mangeot 1
2 Three part Fantasies arr. Warlock 1
Reger Ami Op77b 1
Roussel 1
Schubert Bfl (1817) 3
Stradella-Boghen Toccata 1
Stevens, B. Lyric Suite Op30 (1959) 1
Walthew, R. Three Pieces 1
Five Diversions 4

PIANO TRIOS

Arensky, Dmi Op32 9
Austin, E. Suite Op8 1
Bach, F. G 1
Bach, J.S. C 1
Dmi 1
Bargiel Bfl Op37 2
Barley, A. Op11 1
Bax "Elegiac" (1946) 1
Beethoven Efl Op1 No1 14
G Op1 No2 9

Cmi Op1 No3 29
D Op70 No1 30
Efl Op70 No2 18
Bfl Op97 29
G Op121a 8
Behm Emi Op14 1
Bohm 2
Bennett, S. A Op26 10
Bloch Three Nocturnes 2
Brahms B Op8 2
B Op8r 8
C Op87 25
Cmi Op101 29
Bredt, A.V. Cmi 1
Bridge, F. Cmi 6
Bronsart Cmi Op1 1
Chaminade Ami Op34 1
Chausson 1
Chopin Gmi Op8 1
Cooke, Arnold 1
Couperin A 1
Cusins Cmi Op1 1
Dalby 1
Dunhill Efl Op36 1
Dvořák Bfl Op21 5
Gmi Op26 6
Fmi Op65 15
Emi Op90 20
Erlebach, P.H. 1
Ersfeld 1
Fauré Dmi Op120 1
Fesca, A. Emi Op12 2
F Op54 1
Gade Op29 Novelletten 7
F Op42 11
Godard Emi Op32 1
Goetz Gmi Op1 8
Goldmark Bfl Op4 1
Goossens E Suite Op6 8
2 Impressions of a holiday 1
Haydn G No1 17
Fsh mi No2 2
C No3 5
E No4 3
Efl No5 2
Efl No8 2
A No9 1
Efl No20 1
Efl mi No28 1
D No30 1
C 1
Bfl 2
Hummel Efl Op12 2
Hurlstone G 3
Ireland E No3 1
Ami Phantasy 4
Jensen Op27 1
Jongen, Joseph Bmi Op10 3
Bmi Op30 3
Juon, P. Ami Op17 2
Kiel Csh mi Op33 1
Laloux, F. D 1
Lekeu, G. Cmi 1
Loeillet G 1
Bmi 1
Macfarren A 1
Martin, Frank 1
Mathias Op30 1
Mendelssohn Dmi Op49 19
Cmi Op66 15
Moore Variations on a French Nursery Tune 1
Mozart Bfl K502 7
E K542 10
C K548 8
G K564 6
Sinfonia Concertante arr. Vn Va Pf K364 1
O'Neill, N. F Op32 1
Parry Bmi 2
Emi 3
Piston, Walter (1939) 1
Raff Cmi Op102 1
G Op112 4
Ravel Ami 12
Reber Efl Op12 1
Reinecke Ami Op118 1
Reissiger F Op25 1
Rheinberger A Op112 4
Rubbra Op68 (1 movement) 2
Rubinstein Gmi Op15 1
Bfl Op52 6
Saint-Saëns F Op18 12
Sarasate 2
Schubert Bfl D898 34
Efl D929 19
Efl D897 3
Bfl (1 movement) 2
Schumann Dmi Op63 17
F Op80 8
Ami Op88 17
Gmi Op110 4
Schütt Cmi Op27 4
Emi Op51 1
Op72 1
Shostakovich Op67 2
Sinding Op56 1
C Op87 1
Smetana Gmi Op15 9
Spohr Bmi Op88 No1 2
Stanford Efl Op35 1
Gmi Op73 1
Irish Concertino Op161 3
Swepstone, E. Dmi 1
Gmi 1
Ami 1
Tchaikovsky Ami Op50 16
Turner, B Cmi 1
Turina No1 2
No2 Bmi Op76 1
Walenn, F. Miniature Trio 1
Walthew, R. D 5
G 9
Warner, W. Ami Op22 1
Wilm Emi Op165 1

UNCLASSIFIED TRIOS

Bach Concerto Fl Vn
  Pf Ami 3
  Sonata in C Fl Vn
  Con 1
  Musical Offering
  Fl Vn Hpchd Cmi 1
  Vn Vn Vc A 1
  Vn Vn Vc Bmi 1
Bartók Contrasts
  Cl Vn Pf 1
Beethoven Bfl Op11
  Pf Cl Vc 16
  D Op25 Fl Vn Va 18
Boccherini Vn Vn Pf 1
Brahms Efl Op40 Pf
  Vn H 21
  Ami Op114 Pf Cl
  Vc 18
Couperin Cmi F Vn
  Cont 1
Debussy Gmi 1916
  Fl Va Hp 4
Françaix Divertisse-
  ment Ob Cl Bn 1
Haydn D Fl Vn pf 1
  No30 Fl Vn Vc 1
  Vn Vn Pf 1
Holbrooke Horn Trio
  D Op36 2
Leclair D Op2 Fl Va Hp 1
Milhaud Suite Ob Cl Bn
  D'après Corrette 1
Mozart Efl K498 Pf
  Cl Va 11
  Pf Vn Va 3
Ponchielli Cl Cl Pf
  Divertimento 1
Rameau Hpchd
  Viol d'amore gamba 1
Rawsthorne Ami Suite
  Fl Va Hp 1
Reger G Op141a
  Serenade Fl Vn Va 1
Schubert Op132
  Clarinet Trio 3
Spooner Dmi Cl Va Vc 1
Stevens Op38 Pf Hn Vn 1
Uhl Kleines Konzert
  P Cl Va 2
Vivaldi Ami Fl Va Hp 1
Walthew, R. Cmi
  Clarinet Trio 12
Warner, W. D Vn Vn
  Pf Divertimento 6

KEYBOARD & VIOLIN

Akimento Dmi 1
Arne Bfl 1
Austin Poème Op29 1
Bach, J.S. E 2
  Bmi 2
  Cmi 1
  Emi 3
Barth, R. Bmi Op20 1
Bartók No1 1
  No2 3
Bax No2 1
  No3 1
  Ballade 1
Beethoven Op12 No1 3
  Op12 No2 1
  Op12 No3 3
  Ami Op23 3
  F Op24 7
  A Op30 No1 3
  Cmi Op30 No2 14
  G Op30 No3 4
  A Op47 33
  Romance F Op50 1
  G Op96 8
Benjamin, A. B 1
Bloch No1 (1920) 1
  No2 Poème Mystique 1
Brahms G Op78 17
  A Op100 17
  Dmi Op108 18
  Sonatensatz Cmi 7
Catoire 1
Davies, Walford Emi
  Op5 1
Debussy 4
Delius No1 1
  No2 2
  No3 1
Dohnanyi Csh mi Op21 9
Dvořák F Op57 3
  G Op100 5
Elgar Emi Op82 8
Farjeon, H. Efl Op69 1
Fauré A Op13 1
  Emi Op108 1
Franck A 23
Fuchs, R. 5 Inter-
  mezzi Op40 1
Gade Dmi Op21 4
Gibbs Dmi 1
  Op63 1
Goossens No2 1
Grieg F Op8 13
  G Op13 10
  Cmi Op45 12
Halvorsen Suite 1
Handel A 3
  D 4
  E 2
Harty, H. Irish Fantasy 1
Hinton, A. Op20 1
Holland D Op47 1
Holbrooke, J. Op6 1
  F Op59 1
Howells, H. E 1
Ireland No1 Dmi 1
  No2 Ami 4
Janáček 1
Josten, W. 1
Leclair No3 D 1
Lekeu G 6
McEwen Sonata
  Fantasia 1
Medtner Bmi Op21 2
Mendelssohn Op4 1
Moeran Emi 1

Morris O'Connor
Irish Sonata 1
Mozart Bfl K15 1
C K296 1
G K301 3
Emi K304 4
D K306 2
F K376 2
Bfl K378 4
G K379 2
Efl K380 4
A K402 1
Bfl K454 5
Efl K481 2
A K526 5
F K547 1
Nardini D 1
Parry Dmi 1
Pierné Op36 1
Pijper No1 (1919) 1
Pizzetti A 1
Prokofiev No2 A Op94 2
Purcell Gmi 2
Ravel G (1927) 1
Reizenstein G (1945)
Respighi Bmi 2
Rubinstein Op13 1
Saint-Saëns Dmi Op75 3
Schmitt Sonate Libre 1
Schubert Rondo
Brillant Bmi Op70 9
Gmi Op137 No3 1
C Op159 5
Introduction & variations on an original theme
Op160 1
Op162 4
Schumann Op73 4
Ami Op105 5
Dmi Op121 8
Schütt Op61 1
Seiber 1
Sjoren Emi Op24 3
Stanford Op54 1
Jig and Reel 1
Hush Song & Jig 1
6 Irish Fantasies 2
Stoker Op15 1
Strauss, R. Efl Op18 2
Tartini Gmi 4
Trowell G Op24 1
Villa-Lobos lst Sonata 1
Vreuls B 1
Walker, E. Ami Variations on a theme of Joachim 1
Walthew, R. Afl 6
Sonata in G 1
Wood-Smith Miniatures 1
Zimmerman Dmi Op16 1

PIANO AND VIOLA

Benjamin, A. 1
Bloch Suite 2
Boccherini A 10
Bowen, York Op1 1
Hindemith 1
Proctor, C. Fmi 1
Richardson Sussex Lullaby 1
Schumann Op113 4
Vaughan Williams Suite Group 1 1
Walker, E. C Op29 2
Walthew, R. Fmi 2
D 1
Winkler Op10 1

KEYBOARD AND VIOLONCELLO

Bach, J.S. No2 D 2
G 2
Bax 1
Beethoven F Op5 No1 3
Gmi Op5 No2 2
A Op69 6
C Op102 No1 1
D Op102 No2 3
12 variations on a theme from Judas Maccabeus 4
Bloch Voices in the Wilderness 1
Boëllmann Ami Op40 4
Brahms Emi Op38 11
F Op99 5
Bridge, F. Dmi 1
Chopin C Op3 10
Debussy Dmi 4
Delius 1
Dohnanyi Bfl Op8 4
Eccles Gmi 1
Farjeon, H. D 1
Fauré No2 1
Elegy 1
Goldmark F Op39 1
Goossens, E. Rhapsody Op13 1
Grieg Ami Op36 5
Handel Gmi 2
Hindemith Op25 No3 1
Hure, J. Fsh mi 2
Hurlstone E 1
Ireland Gmi 2
Jongen Poem 1
Kodaly Op4 2
Martinu Variations on a Theme by Rossini 1
Mendelssohn D Op17 9
Bfl Op45 3
D Op58 5
Napravnik Romance 1
Nin Suite Espagnole 1
Nunn, W. 1
Rubinstein D Op18 4
Rubbra Gmi Op60 2
Rachmaninov G Op19 1

Saint-Saëns Cmi Op32 1
Sammartini G 2
Schubert Ami Arpeggione 1
Schumann Op70 2
Op73 Phantasiestück 6
Op102 1
Stanford D Op39 1
Valentini E 1
Walthew, R. D 2
Weber Duo 1

PIANO AND BASSOON

Hurlstone F 1

PIANO AND CLARINET

Bax 1
Brahms Fmi Op120 No1 2
Efl Op120 No2 9
Debussy 1st Rhapsody 2
Hamilton, Iain 1
Howells Comdey Suite 1
Hurlstone Four Pieces 1
Poulenc 1
Reger Bfl Op107 1
Samuel, H. 3 Light Pieces 1
Walthew, R. Mosaic in 10 Pieces 3
Suite 3
Four Meditations 2
Meditations 2nd set 1
Weber Efl Op48 3

PIANO AND FLUTE

Bach, J.S. E 2
Godard 1
Handel Ami 1

PIANO AND HORN

Beethoven F Op17 2
Fricker Op24 1
Hindemith 1

DUET FOR TWO PIANOS

Arensky Polonaise and Romance 2
Op15 3
Silhouettes 1
Waltz 1
Bach, J.C. Sonata in G 1
Concerto in C 1
Bax Moy Mell 1
Hardanger 1
The Poisoned Fountain 1
Brahms Haydn Variations Op56b 10
Busoni Duettino Concertante 1
Chabrier Valse 1
Bourée fantastique 1
Clementi Sonata in Bfl 1
Debussy En Blanc et noir 1
D'Erlanger 3
Farnaby Piece for 2 Virginals 1
Glière Les Nymphes 1
Nocturne 2
Mazurka 1
Air de Ballet 1
Granados Malagueña 1
Hahn, F. Pour bercer un convalescent 1
Handel Arrival of the Queen of Sheba (arr.) 1
Infante Manuele Ritmo 3
Spanish Dance 4
Gracia 1
Lecuona Malagueña 1
McEwen, J. 1
Melon-Gueroult Tourbillon 2
Milhaud Scaramouche 1
Mozart A K305 1
D K448 1
F K497 2
D 6
Fmi K608 arr. Busoni 1
O'Neill Variations and Fugue on an Irish Theme Op17 3
Palmgren The Black Domino 1
Rachmaninov Suite Op17 3
Rosenbloom Variations & Fugue in Bfl 1
Rudorff Op1 1
Saint-Saëns Variations on a Beethoven theme 2
Study in Thirds 1
Schubert D Rondo Op138 1
Marche caractér--istique 1
Andantino varié Op84 No1 2
Schumann Andante and Variations Op46 3
Study in Canon Form Ami 2
Schmitt, F. Rhapsodie Viennoise Op53 No3 1
Sinding Op2 Variations 1
Andante 1
Vuillemin Bourée and Pavane Op16 1
Ysaÿe, T. Variations and Caprice 1

PIANO DUETS

Ashton, A. 1
Brahms 1
Bizet 1
Delius 2
Bowen, Y. 1
Dvořák 1
Farjeon, H. 1
Grieg 1
Jensen 1
Juon 1
Mendelssohn 3
Moszkowski 1
Mozart Variations
  G K501 2
  F K497 1
Nicodé 1
Schubert Fmi Fantasia
  Op103 7
  Grand duo C Op140 2
Schumann 1
Sinding 1
Svendsen 1

PIANO AND DOUBLE BASS

Bottesini Elegy and
  Tarantella 1

TWO VIOLINS

Godard Op18 No1 1
Pugnani Sonata in C 1
Purcell Golden Sonata 1
Spohr Op67 No2 1

VIOLIN AND VIOLA

Mozart G K423 3
  Bfl K424 2
Spohr Emi Op13

VIOLIN AND CELLO

Bottesini 1
Handel Passacaglia 5
Honegger Sonatina
  1932 1
Ravel 1
Swain, F. 1

VIOLIN AND HARP

Saint-Saëns Op124 1
Spohr Efl Op113 1

VIOLIN AND ORGAN

Vitali Chaconne 1

WORKS FOR SOLO INSTRUMENTS AND ORCHESTRA

otherwise unclassified

Bach
Brandenburg Concerto No4 (2Fl Vn) 1
Brandenburg Concerto No5 (Fl Vn Hpschd) 4
Concerto Dmi (Ob Vn St Orch) 1
Boccherini Cello Concerto Bfl 1
Brahms Concerto (Vn Vc) Op102 1
Fricker
Concertante (Cor Ang St Orch) 1
Handel
Concerto (Hp St Orch) Op4 No6 1
Haydn
Sinfonia Concertante (Vn Ob Vc Bn) 1
Holst
Fugal Concerto (Fl Ob St Orch) 1
Mozart
Sinfonia Concertante (Vn Va) Efl (K364) 2
Horn Concerto No3 Efl (K447) 1
Quantz Flute Concerto 1
Stamitz Clarinet Concerto 1
Strauss, R. Oboe Concerto 1
Telemann Viola Concerto G 1
Valensin Menuet (Vc St Orch) 1
Wall, A. Ballade (Va St Orch) 1

OVERTURES

Auber
Fra Diavolo 1
Le Domino Noir 1
Beethoven Leonora C No1 Op138 1
Bennett, S. The Naiades Op15 1
Delibes Le Roi L'a dit 2
Gluck Iphigenia auf Aulis 1
Gounod Mirella 2
Mendelssohn
Calm sea & Prosperous voyage 1
Son and Stranger 2
Mozart
Così fan tutte 1
Il Seraglio 1
La Clemenza di Tito 1
La Vilanella Rapita 3
Rossini La Gazza Ladra 1
Schumann Genoveva 1
Smetana Der Kuss 1
Stanford Shamus O'Brien 1
Strauss, J. Die Fledermaus 1
Walthew, R. Friend Fritz 1

SYMPHONIES

Beethoven No2 D 1
Dvořák No8 G 2
Goetz F 1
Gounod Efl 1
Haydn
Fsh mi No45 (Farewell) 1
Efl No99 (London No10) 1
D No101 1
Bfl No102 1
Mendelssohn No4 (Italian) 1
Mozart
No33 Bfl (K319) 1
No35 (K385) 1
Schubert No5 Bfl 1
Schumann
No1 Bfl 1
No2 C 1
No4 D 1

OTHER ORCHESTRAL WORKS

Delibes Suite "Le Roi s'amuse" 1
Fauré "Masques et Bergamasques" 1
Findlay "Intermezzo" 1
Glinka Fantasy "Komarinskaja 1
Gluck Ballet music "Paris & Helen" 1
Godard Suite "Scènes Poetiques" 1
Messager "Passepied" 1
Wagner "Siegfried Idyll" 1
Walthew Suite "The Masqueraders" 1

CONCERTOS FOR PIANO AND ORCHESTRA

Arne (arr Herbage)
(piano and string orch) 1
Bach
E 1
Dmi 8
Beethoven
No1 C 1
No3 Cmi 1
Grieg Ami Op16 1
Haydn D Op21 2
Head, M. In one movement 1
Mozart
A (K414) 3
Efl (K449) 2
Turina Rapsodia Sinfonia 3
Walthew, R.
Fiammetta (Concert Piece) 2

CONCERTOS FOR VIOLIN AND ORCHESTRA

Bach
Ami 3
Dmi (two violins) 4
E 4
Bruch Gmi 1
Beethoven Romance in F Op50 1
Corelli La Folia 1
Mozart
No3 G 1
No5 A 1
Nardini Emi 1
Saint-Saëns
Introduction &
Rondo Capriccioso 1
Telemann (four violins) 1
Vivaldi
Ami 1
Bmi (four violins) 3
Dmi (two violins) 2
"Winter" from "The Seasons" 1

STRING ORCHESTRA

Addison, John Partita 1
Arne-Rawlinson Aria & Giga 1
Aubert Père-Collins Tambourin 1
Avison Concerto Emi 1
Bach
Brandenburg Concerto No3 3
Brandenburg Concerto No6 1
Bartók
Divertimento 2
Rumanian Folk Dances 3
Beaumont, A. Menuet de la Reine 1
Bliss Music for strings 1
Bloch
Concerto Grosso
(piano Obbligato) 1
Boyce Symphony Bfl 1
Britten
Variations on a theme of Frank
Bridge 1
Corelli
Concerto Grosso Op6 No7 D 1
Concerto Grosso Op6 No8 Gmi 4
Delius
Air & Dance 1
Two Aquarelles 1
Dvořák Serenade E Op22 4
Elgar
Introduction & Allegro Op47
(St Qt & St Orch) 4
Serenade Op20 2
Galuppi Adagio & Gigue 1
Geminiani Concerto Grosso Cmi 1
Grainger
Irish Reel "Molly on the shore" 1
Grieg
Elegiac melodies Op34 2
Holberg suite 1
Two Norwegian melodies Op63 1
Handel
Concerto Grosso Op6 No7 1
Concerto Grosso Op6 No11 3
Concerto Grosso Op6 No12 1
Overture to Faramondo 1
Holst St Paul's Suite 1
Ireland, J. Concertino Pastorale 1

Lalo Two aubades	1
Mozart	
Divertimento D (K136)	3
Divertimento Bfl (K137)	1
Divertimento F (K138)	2
Serenata Notturno D (K239)	2
Serenade G (K525)	1
Adagio and Fugue Cmi	1
Pergolesi	
Concerto No3 E	1
Concerto No4 Fmi	1
Purcell Chaconne Gmi	2
Rameau-Cundell Suite	1
Rameau-Savage Suite	1
Respighi Ancient Airs & Dances	1
Rooper, J. Sinfonia	1
Rossini Sonata No1 G	2
Sandby, H. Swedish folk song	1
Sibelius	
Canzonetta	1
Romance C	4
Swepstone, E.	
Idyll "Woods in April"	1
Taylor, Coleridge Dance Nègre	1
Tchaikovsky Serenade Op48	5
Vaughan Williams	
Partita for Double St Orch	1
Warlock, P. "Capriol Suite"	1
Weiner, Leo Suite of Czech Dances	1

CHAMBER ORCHESTRA

Bach	
Suite in D	1
Suite in Bmi	3
Dvořák Serenade Dmi Op44	
(2Ob 2Cl 2Bn 3Hn Vc Db)	2

INSTRUMENTAL SOLOS

Programmes have included solos on the following instruments. The figure in brackets indicates the number of different composers whose works have been performed:

Bassoon (1), Cello (116), Clarinet (6), Double bass (1), Flute (8), Harp (7), Harpsichord (7), Horn (2), Oboe (4), Organ (1), Piano (148), Violin (165), Viola (15), Viol d'Amore (1).

VOCAL QUARTETS, DUETS AND SOLOS

Programmes have included works from the sixteenth century up to the present. Details of the more important works are given.

Bach, J.S. Cantate No82 Ich habe genug (2)
Beethoven An die ferne Geliebte Op98 (5)
Berg Sieben frühe Lieder (1)
Brahms Acht Zigeunerlieder Op163 (1)
Liebeslieder Walzer (2)
Neue Liebesliederwalzer (2)
Britten Les Illuminations (1)
Seven Songs of Michelangelo (2)
Six Hölderlin Fragments Op39 (1)
Still falls the Rain (1)
The Holy Sonnets of John Donne Op35 (1)
Who are these Children? (1)
Winter Words (2)

Butterworth A Shropshire Lad (1)
Chandler The Time of Waiting (1)
Fauré La Bonne Chanson (2)
Finzi Seven Songs for High Voice (1)
Henschel Serbisches Liederspiel (1)
Moeran Seven Poems of James Joyce (2)
Mozart Eine kleine deutsche Kantate K619 (2)
Quilter To Julia (Herrick) (1)
Schönberg Pierrot Lunaire (2)
Schubert Auf dem Strom (1)
Der Hirt auf dem Felsen Op129 (7)
Die schöne Müllerin Op25 (10)
Schwanengesang (3)
Winterreise Op89 (8)
Schumann Dichterliebe Op48 (6)
Frauenliebe und Leben (4)
Gedichte der Königin Maria (1)
Liederkreis von Eichendorff (4)
Liederkreis von Heine Op24 (1)
Spanische Liebeslieder (1)
Twelve Poems by Kerner Op35 (1)
Somervell A Shropshire Lad (2)
Twelve Songs from Maud (3)
Stanford A Fire of Turf (2)
Four Songs of a roving Celt (1)
Irish Idyll (2)
Tippett Boyhood's End (1)
The Heart's Assurance (2)
Vaughan Williams On Wenlock Edge (4)
The House of Life (1)
Wolf Four Songs of Mignon (1)

The total number of composers represented is 816

ENSEMBLES

PIANO TRIOS

Archduke (1972)	1
Arieli (1969)	1
Arieli-Pini (1957)	1
Bartholdy (1975)	1
Bentwich (1915-18)	4
Blech (1940	1
Bohr-Egerton-Ould (1895)	1
Boise (1967)	1
Bowman (1957)	1
Bradley (1887-90)	8
Bright (1890)	1
Bronkhurst (1947)	1
Budapest (1952)	1
Busch (1935)	1
Canadian (1932-38)	5
Chaplin (1887-1914)	25
Clifford (1899)	1
Cohen (1980)	1
Cole (1935)	4
Defauw (1915-22)	5
Dettmar Dressel (1929-30)	2
Dulcken (1900-02)	3
Dumka (1961-68)	7
English (1920-21)	2
Epstein-Bentwich (1912-13)	2
Fairhurst (1946)	1
Fellowes (1907-11)	7
Ferguson-Kersey-Just (1931)	1
Fisher (1932)	1
Fryer-Zimmermann-Ludwig (1910)	1
Gabrieli (1965)	1
Gainsborough (1983-86)	2
Gates (1891-1908)	6
Grimson (1896-1923)	8
Grinke (1938)	2
Gruenberg (1960)	1
Harmonic (1918-25)	3

Harry Isaacs (1945-61) 15
Harty (1902) 1
Hobday (1917-34) 2
Ionian (1930) 1
Ireland-Langley-Sharpe (1914) 1
Kamaran (1938-45) 3
Kantrovitch (1957-67) 4
Klein-Zacharewitsch-Sissermann (1926) 1
Kutcher (1923) 1
Levey-Carter-Crabb (1898) 1
Littmann-Walenn-Werg (1899) 1
Loveday (1950) 1
Loveridge-Martin-Hooton (1951) 1
Maitlant-Such-Renard (1904) 1
Martin (1965-69) 3
Morrison-Eaton-Butler (1935) 1
Neaman (1956) 1
Nelson (1956) 1
New English (1934-35) 1
New (1905-11) 10
O'Connor-Morris-Eaton-Salmond (1919) 1
Orion (1975) 1
Oromonte (1966) 1
Parikian-Fleming-Roberts 1977-83) 7
Parikian-Milne-Fleming (1985) 1
Paul (1921) 2
Pecker (1925) 1
Pirani (1928-38) 4
Plimmer-Cobbett-Hann (1889) 1
Polanski (1887-91) 12
Pusey (1888) 1
Reizenstein (1957) 1
Rubbra-Glazier-Pleeth (1947) 1
Rubbra-Gruenberg-Pleeth (1949-53) 5
Samuel-Hayward-Jones (1918) 1
Saunders (1891-1918) 7
St Cecilia (1957-63) 4
Serre (1933) 1
Schiller (1973) 1
Sharpe (1900) 1
Snowden (1922-31) 3
Swain-Kontorovitch-Otscharkoff (1925) 1
Sweetland-Trotter-Friendship (1928) 1
Tononi (1969-71) 2
Trio Players (1932-34) 2
Troup (1889-98) 28
Tunnell (1966) 2
Walenn (1896-98) 5
Walthew (1897-1927) 20
Wessely (1894) 1
Wild-Kummer-Ould (1892-93) 3
Winifred Small (1927) 1
Zingara (1981-83) 2

STRING TRIOS

Arion (1983) 1
British (1935) 1
Carter (1955) 1
Cummings (1978-86) 3
Glickman (1980) 1
International (1928) 1
Oromonte (1960-65) 4
Philharmonic (1935-51) 3
Philharmonic (1975) 1
Rawlins (1920-29) 5
Richards (1980-82) 2
Saunders (1915) 1

UNCLASSIFIED TRIOS

Cembalo (Hpchd Vn Vc) (1937) 1
Civil Horn Trio (Hn Vn Pf) (1965) 2
Gabrieli (Cl Vc Pf) (1975) 1
King-Tunnell (Cl Vc Pf) (1985) 1
Robles (Fl Va Hp) 1
Schiller (Vn Hn Pf) (1976-86) 2

PIANO QUARTETS

Bauer (1891) 1
Bradley (1888-92) 6
Chaplin (1911) 1
Cheyne (1888) 1
Defauw (1914-21) 5
Elzy (1920-24) 4

English (1945-51)	2
English (1976)	1
Gates (1888-1901)	5
Grimson (1894-1934)	9
Henkel (1912-28)	5
Imhof (1887-89)	2
Kinsey (1923-25)	2
London (1937-67)	11
Maguire (1965)	1
Masters (1950-63)	16
Meredyll (1921-26)	3
Nemet (1967)	1
Parkin (1926)	1
Parry (1940-60)	2
Paul (1934-38)	4
Phillips (1940)	1
Physick (1887)	2
Plowitz (1892-93)	3
Power (1919)	1
Pro Arte (1963-66)	3
Richards (1946-78)	6
Saunders (1891-1914)	5
Shedlock-Hann (1888-89)	5
Stratton (1929)	1
Troup (1890-1900)	3
Tunnell (1975)	1
Villiers (1985)	1
Walenn (1889-96)	2
Walthew (1894-1933)	28
Wethmar (1940)	1
Woodhouse (1928-33)	2

STRING QUARTETS

Aeolian (1945-69)	58
Alberni (1963-86)	46
Aleph (1949-52)	6
Allegri (1953-87)	41
Allied (1918)	1
Amadeus (1947-69)	11
Amici (1956-85)	63
Amphion (1981-84)	5
Arioso (1978-80)	3
Arriaga (1965-70)	9
Auriol (1985)	1
Backhouse (1921)	1
Barylli (1950-51)	1
Bauer (1891-92)	6
Beel (1902)	1
Bent (1894)	1
Benthien (1953)	1
Bentwich (1918-19)	2
Birmingham Ladies (1936-37)	3
Blagrove (1912)	1
Blech (1934-49)	25
Blower (1929)	1
Bochmann (1977-87)	16
Bowmann (1928)	1
British (1915-36)	4
British Women's (1930-31)	2
Brosa (1926-38)	16
Brunet (1916-20)	4
Cardiff (University Ensemble) (1966-67)	2
Carl Pini (1972)	1
Cathie (1904-06)	4
Cazaubon (1889)	1
Chilingirian (1971-86)	13
Clayton (1915)	1
Clench (1903-06)	2
Cobbett (1892-1913)	9
Coleman (1919)	1
Coull (1977-85)	12
Croydon (1918)	1
Court (1978)	1
Cummings (1971)	1
Dartington (1961-80)	32
Defauw (1914-17)	10
Delmé (1971-86)	10
Dutch (1952-53)	2
Eaton (1918-37)	2
Edinburgh (1956-84)	14
Egerton (1914)	1
Element (1953-54)	2
Endellion (1980-85)	4
English (1912-13/1920-21)	2
English (1959-86)	23
Entente (1927-46)	10
Fairfield (1983-85)	2
Fitzwilliam (1972-85)	14
Franklin (1929-35)	11
Gabrieli (1967-74)	7
Gates (1888-98)	3
Georgian (1968-75)	18
Gibbs (1949-52)	8
Grace Thynne (1923)	1
Griller (1929-45)	34
Grimson (1896-1934)	33

Guadagnini (1979-81)	2
Haffner (1968-75)	16
Hann (1889-90)	11
Hanson (1979-86)	8
Hayward (1919-49)	3
Henkel (1887-90)	7
Hesse (1933)	1
Hirsch (1938-60)	58
Hurwitz (1946-49)	11
International (1931-38)	6
Jupiter (1971-74)	3
Kantrovitch (1946-53)	7
Kendall (1923)	1
Kersey (1930)	1
Kinsey (1918-24)	6
Kinze (1913-16)	3
Koeckert (1951)	1
Kutcher (1920-26)	9
Ladies' (1923)	1
Langley (1908-12)	3
Lindsay (1970-87)	17
Locrian (1980-86)	6
Loewenguth (1948)	1
London (New London) (1956-80)	37
McGibbon (1936-69)	19
Mangeot (1934)	1
Manoliu (1952)	1
Martin (1946-69)	37
Mandeville (1922)	1
M'Cullugh (1922)	1
Medici (1973-79)	7
Menges (1935-46)	8
Metropolitan (1931)	1
Miles (1898)	1
Modern (1921-22)	2
New English (1933-38)	6
New Philharmonic (1926-27)	2
New (1909-26)	10
Newcastle (1981)	1
Ould (1891)	2
Palmer (1896)	1
Parisian (1913)	1
Pecker (1924)	1
Pennington (1920-21)	4
Philharmonia (1949)	1
Philharmonic (1930–51)	6
Phillips (1929-38)	6
Pollitzer (1888-89)	2
Pro Musica (1957-60)	8
Quartet of London (1978-85)	5
Rasoumovsky (1975-79)	7
Rawlins (1928-46)	16
Reed (1913-22)	3
Regimental (1917)	1
Röntgen (1952-53)	2
Rooke (1895)	1
Roth (1984-87)	2
Ryerson (1934)	1
Salomon (1983)	1
Sartori (1972-75)	2
Saunders (1891-1918)	204
Schwiller (1910-35)	23
Sebastian (1953)	1
Shinner (1895)	1
Sissermann (1924)	1
Slocombe (1893-95)	5
Snow (1921-27)	2
Spencer Dyke (1919-35)	15
Spivac (1923)	1
Stratton (1935-38)	26
Sturdy (1947-49)	3
Sutton (1888)	1
Turner (1936-50)	3
Van Heuvel (1937)	1
Vegh (1950)	1
Walenn (1888-97)	29
Wang (1954-62)	10
Wayfaring (1921-23)	4
Wessely (1899-1910)	19
Whinyates (1931-40)	10
Wigmore (1947)	1
Willoughby (1936)	1
Wilson (1927-45)	11
Winifred Small (1922)	1
Woodhouse (1905-33)	22
Wood-Smith (1922-28)	18
Zorian (1945-48)	4

UNCLASSIFIED ENSEMBLES

Allegri-Robles (1977-80)	2
Brain Wind (1948-54)	2
Cameristi of London (1979)	1
Capricorn (1981)	1
Consort of Musick (1982)	1
Dartington (1984)	1
Divertimenti (1982-86)	2

English Chamber Music Players (1951) 1
Ensemble Players (1930) 3
Gabrieli Ensemble (1966) 1
Grimson Octet (1895-1900) 9
Jaye Consort (1975-81) 2
King's Musick (1978-82) 2
London Festival Players (1981-86) 5
London Harpsichord Ensemble (1951-72) 2
London Octet (1964-67) 2
Melos Ensemble (1953-69) 14
Meridian (1976) 1
Music Group of London (1969) 1
Nash (1972) 1
New London Wind Ensemble (1973-77) 2
Northern Sinfonia (1969-75) 3
Oboe Quartet (1970-77) 3
Oromonte Ensemble (1983) 1
Portia Wind Ensemble (1961) 1
Prometheus Ensemble (1957) 1
Schubert Ensemble of London (1986) 1
Tilford Festival Ensemble (1970-81) 11
Vesuvius (1977) 1
Virtuoso Ensemble (1959-72) 10
Virtuoso Wind Quintet (1946) 1
Whitehead Chamber Music Group (1949) 1

STRING AND CHAMBER ORCHESTRAS

Birmingham Philharmonic String Orchestra (1936) 1
Boyd Neel String Orchestra (1934) 1
Brain Chamber Orchestra (1955) 1
Camerata String Orchestra (1967) 1
City String Players (1935-37) 1
Harvey Phillips String Orchestra (1935) 1
Hirsch Chamber Players (1960-62) 2
Hurwitz Chamber Ensemble (1954-62) 5
Informal Chamber Orchestra (1946-47) 2
London Women's String Orchestra (1938-40) 2
Morley College String Orchestra (1948) 1
Riddick String Orchestra (1949-52) 3

INSTRUMENTALISTS

Mesdames

Adam, Marjorie
Adami
Aldis, Maud E.
Allan, Winifred
Alleyne, Iris
Amberg, Marie-Luise
Amherst, Elwyn
Angove, Ivy
Ansermier, Eugénie
Arajo, Ruth
Arieli, Celia
Arnaud, Yvonne
Arnold, Hildegard
Ashby, Edith
Aspinall, Dorothea
Attwell, Jessie
Attwood, Ethel
Backhouse, Rhoda
Baker, Gertrude
Barrett, May
Barrett, Nerine
Barrie, Dorothy
Bartlett, Ethel
Basche, Lonie
Batchelor, Nora K.
Bateman, Alice
Bateson, Margaret
Bauer, Ethel
Bauer, Winifred
Beamish, Sally
Beard, Rosemary
Bedlington, Isabel
Beech, Daisy
Bellaby
Bennett, Ruth
Bentwich, Margery
Bentwich, Thelma
Berridge, Enid
Berry, Gwen
Biret, Idil
Black, Laura
Blackmore, Aida
Bligh, Eldina
Bloom, Olive
Bloom, Tessa
Blower, Molly
Boenders, Elizabeth
Bolton, Hetty
Bond, Emily
Bor, Hilda
Borland, Rosalind
Bosworth, Ina
Bourne, Una
Bowater, Jessie
Bower, Jacqueline
Bowley, Marion
Bowley, Winifred
Braham, Editha
Brain, Muriel
Braus, Dorothea
Brereton, Flora
Bridburg, Ruth
Bridson, Dorothy
Briggs, Helen R.
Bright, Dora
Brook, Dorothy
Brown, Josephine
Browning, Dorothy
Bucknall, Joan
Bucktrout, Daisy
Bull, Leila
Burdess, Kay
Burgess, Mary
Burrows, Grace
Butler, Antonia
Byrne, Olive
Caine, E.N.
Callender, Dorothy
Camden, Joyce
Candy, Elsie
Carbutt, Diana
Carmichael, Mary
Carr, Marietta
Carelle, Beatrice
Carter, Mary
Cassidy, Patsy
Cassola, M.
Catterall, Yvonne
Cave, Ethel
Chalmers, Dorothy
Chamberlain, Margaret
Chaplin, Hubbard
Chaplin, Kate
Chaplin, Mabel
Chaplin, Nellie
Charleson, Elizabeth
Cheverton, Una
Cheyne, Kate
Child, Cecilia
Chilley, Marion
Chilton-Griffin
Christie, May
Christie, Winifred
Christison, Dorothea
Churton, Edith
Clark, Joyce McGown
Clarke, Gladys
Clarke, Rebecca
Clayton, Dorothea
Cleaver, Sylvia
Clements, Dora
Cleminson, Nicola
Clench, Nora
Clifford, Colleen
Clifford, Elsa
Coates, Kate
Cochrane, Margaret
Coetmore, Peers
Cohen, Harriet
Colam, Mildred
Cole, Annette
Cole, Winifred
Collier, Marian
Comberti, Michaela
Conroy, Madge
Cooke, Eleanor
Cooke, Evelyn
Cooke, Madge
Cooper, Imogen
Cooper, Nem
Copeland, Sybil

Instrumentalists (contd.)

Copperwheat, Winifred
Cosma, Sofia
Coupe, Margaret
Courtnedge, Phyllis
Cover, Lily
Cowen, Margaret
Cracroft, Mary
Craxton, Janet
Crayford, Marcia
Creffield, Florence
Croft, Peggy
Crouch, Ruth
Crowden, Anne
Croxford, Eileen
Crum, Alison
Cummings, Diana
Cunningham, Sara
Darley, Mary
Darlington, Dorothy
Davenport, Muriel
Davey, Jean
Davey, Juliet
Davey, Winifred
David, Violette
Davidson, Olive
Davies, Arvon
Davies, Cecilia
Davies, Joan
Davies, Joan Rochfert
Davies, Kate Augusta
Davies, Llewela
Davies, Phyllipa
Davies, Sylvia
Davis, Eleanor
D'Aranyi, Jelly
Dawson, Constance
Dean, Ivy
Dechaume, Cécile G.
DeGay, Sylvia
Defauw, Jeanne
Delias, Alannah
Desbruslais, Julia
Dickson, Joan
Dixon, Cecile
Dixon, Maude
Dobree, Georgina
Doenau, Topsie
Dolmetsch, Hélène
Donne, Muriel
Dorey, Susan
Dossor, Mary
Doubleday, Leila
Down, Daphne
Dulcken, Mar
Duncan, Miriam
Dundas-Grant, Deirdre
Du Val, Lorraine
Dyer, Queenie
Dyson, Ruth
Eades, Mary
Eaton, Sybil
Edes, Marjorie
Egerton, Helen
Ehrlich, Ruth
Eitler, Marta
Elmitt, Mavis
Elphick, Edna
Engelbrecht, Eileen
Esterson, Kitty
Evans, Irene Frances
Evans, Lilian
Evans, Maud F.
Everitt, Dorothy
Fachiri, Adila
Fachiri, Adrienne
Fairfax, Margaret
Fairhurst, Adeline
Fairless, Margaret
Falshaw, Nora
Faultless, Margaret
Findley, Gillian
Fishbein, Miriam
Fisher, Ester
Fisher-Sobell
Flack, Nell
Flatter, Hilde
Fleming, Amaryllis
Florence, Vera
Ford, Nora
Forman, Dora
Fourmy, Ruth
Franklin, Rowena
Fraser, Dorothea
Friendship, Barbara
Fry, Annie C.
Fuchsova, Liza
Fullard, Christobel
Fulleylove, Margaret
Gainsborough, Golda
Gapin, Marguerite
Gardiner, Florence
Gardiner, Winifred
Gates, Cecilia
Geisler-Schubert
Geoffroy-Dechaume, Cécile
Geselschap, Marie
Gladden, Mary
Glover, Phoebe
Godfrey, Margaret
Godlee, Rachel
Godson, Jennifer
Gold, Maude
Good, Margaret
Goodwin, Amina
Gotch, Veronica
Gothard, Dora
Gough, Helen
Grady, Edith
Graham, Breta
Graham, Joanna
Graham, May
Grainger, Eileen
Grassie, Alice
Gray, Isabel
Gray, Peggy
Greenbaum, Kyla
Greenhill, Edith O.
Greenish, Doris
Griffith, Mrs Yeatman
Griffiths, Doris
Griffiths, Gwendoline
Grimaldi
Grimson, Amy
Grimson, Annie
Grimson, Jessie

Instrumentalists (contd.)

Grimson, Nellie
Gruenberg, Joanna
Guillain, Kimby
Gunn, Marjorie
Hall, Elsie
Hall, Joy
Hallet, Beatrice
Hambourg, Hope
Handley, Muriel
Hann, Mrs Clement
Hanson, Edith
Hardy, June
Harper, Maude
Hart, Perry
Hartley, Phyllis
Harvey-Samuel, M.
Haselden, Tessa
Hasluck, Phyllis
Hast, Marian
Hatton, Veronica
Hatzfeld, Edna
Hawkins, Bessie
Haynes, Esme
Hayward, Marjorie
Healey, Alice
Hearne, Isabel
Heath, Louie
Hegedus, Olga
Heinitz, Viva
Hemming, Dorothy
Hemmings, Florence
Henderson
Henkel, Lily
Henkel, Vera
Henry, Fraser
Henschel, Helen
Hepple, Dorothy
Herbert, Ita
Herbert, Ivy
Herbert, Muriel
Herman, Joyce
Hess, Myra
Hesse, Dorothy
Hesse, Emmie
Hesse, Ursula
Heyman, Katherine
Higham, Gwendolen
Hill, Judy
Hilton, Janet
Hinchcliffe, Jessie
Hind, Evelyn
Hirstfield, Isabel
Hjort, Kirsti
Hobday, Ethel
Hoby, Constance
Hogben, Dorothy
Holten, Karen
Hood, Florence
Hooton, Florence
Hope, May
Hopkins, Gertrud
Hopkins, Mavis
Horder, Josephine
Houghton, Lunda
Howard, Rosamund
Howard, Penelope
Howe, Frances
Hucknell, Beatrice
Humby, Betty
Humphress, Lily
Hunt, Tamara
Hunter, Evelyn
Hurwitz, Kay
Hutchinson, Joan
Hwass, Tora
Hyman, Jenny
Ibbott, Daphne
Iles, Edna
Inglis, Hazel
Inoué, Yuko
Ireland, Beryl
Isserlis, Rachel
Ivimey, Ella
Izard, Constance
Izard, Margaret
Jamieson, Nannie
Jay, Marian
Jeffreys, Mary
Jenkinson, Rosamund
Jermyn, Ivy
John, Dorothy
John, Josephine
Jones, A.M.
Jones, Adeline
Jones, Auriol
Jones, Dorothy
Joyce, Eileen
Juler, Pauline
Just, Helen
Kaine, Carmel
Kanevskaya, Lilia
Kantrovitch, Vera
Katz, Myrtle
Keady, Emily
Keay, Jan
Kelsey, Carda
Kemp, Amy
Kendall, Katherine
Kennedy, Daisy
Kersey, Eda
Kersey, Rosalie
Kiek, Bessie
Kimpton, Gwynne
King, Thea
Kitchin, Margaret
Kitching, Frances
Klein, Lydia
Knight, Maralyn
Kohler, Irene
Kontorovitch, Lena
Korchinska, Marie
Kornatzki, Lily von
Kotowska, Adela
Ladd, Edith
Lake, Edith
Lambert, Murray
Langdon, Sophie
Langley, Beatrice
Lasker, Anita
Lassimonne, Denise
Lavers, Marjorie
Lawrence, Thelma
Lawson, Margaret
Layton, Jean
Lee, Dorothy
Lee, Josephine

Instrumentalists (contd.)

Lees, Alice
Le Fevre, Jean
Legge, Pom
Legge, Rhoda
Lehmann, Bernice
Leigh, Mona
Lempfert, Marjorie
Leon, Adelina
Le Sage
Leventon, Kate
Levetus, Daisy
Levison, Anne
Ley, Mrs James
Liddell, Nona
Lidka, Maria
Littmann, Fanny
Lloyd, Helen
Lockwood, Florence
Loeser, Brigitte
Lones, Madge
Long, Kathleen
Long, Mary
Longden, Beatrice
Lonsdale, Eva
Lovelace, Mary
Lovell, Maureen
Loveridge, Iris
Lowenthal, Louise
Loynes, Barbara
Loynes, Dorothy
Luard, Helen
Lucas, Clara
Lucas, Marjorie
Lucas, Miran
Lucas, Patience
Lympany, Moura
Macartney, Jean
Macdonagh, Mary
Macgibbon, Margot
Mackendarick, Sheila
McKinley, Sharon
Mackintosh, Catherine
MacLeod, Chrysetta
Macnaghton, Anne
McCarthy, Eileen
McCarthy, Jean
McCheane, Eileen
M'Cullagh, Isabel
M'Cullagh, Mary
McGown, Joyce
Macnamara, Hilary
Major, Margaret
Malsbury, Angela
Manley, Dorothy
Mapple, Katharine
Marcault, Jacqueline
Markbreiter, F.
Markwell, Kathleen
Marr, Beatrice
Marshall, Sybilla
Martin, Dorothy
Martin, Elsa
Marwood, Catherine
Mason, Gwendoline
Massey, Kathleen
Masters, Rachel
Maturin, Sybil
Meggy, Myrtle
Mellis, Mary
Menges, Isolde
Mercedes, Olivera
Meredyll, Marguerite
Messiter, Christine
Meszaros, Susie
Metcalfe, Mrs. Eric
Milholland, Joanna
Milkina, Nina
Mills, Toni
Milne, Gena
Milne, Helen
Milne-Hume, Barbara
Milner, Dora
Mines, Anatole
Moggridge, Dorothy
Moldawsky, Sonia
Molliter-Meux
Monteith, Mabel
Moody, Deirdre
Moore, Maggie
Moorhouse, Kathleen
Morel, Ella
Morris, Sylvia
Moss, Florence
Moss, May
Mountain, Jeannette
Mukle, Anne
Mukle, May
Munro, Jessie
Murdoch, Mary
Murray, Mrs. Christie
Murray, Margaret
Nelson, Anna
Nelson, Ida
Nelson, Sara
Nemet, Mary
Newsham, Gertrude
Nicholas, Emily
Nickson, Jennifer
Noble, Mary
Norman, Margaret
Noverre, Mary
O'Brien, Catherine
O'Neill, Mrs. Norman
Orde, Valentine
Osmonde, Sheila
Osostowicz, Krystyna
Ould, Kate
Owen, Gwendoline
Owen, Rachel
Pacey, Prudence
Pacey, Prunella
Palmer, Phyllis
Palmer, Violet
Panter, Molly
Parker, Norah
Parkin, Ivy
Parry, Hilda
Partridge, Elizabeth
Partridge, Jennifer
Pattenden, Stella
Pauer, May
Pearl, Ruth
Penso, Irene
Peppin, Geraldine
Peppin, Mary
Percival, Edith

Instrumentalists (contd.)

Perkin, Helen
Pernel, Orrea
Phillips, Jessie
Phillips, Lilly
Phillips, Nancy
Pierrepont, Margaret
Piggott, Audrey
Pirani, Leila
Polakoff, Ania
Pollard, Shirley
Porter, Amy
Powell, Helen
Preston, Pamela
Prior, Hester
Puddy, Maude
Pusey, Violet
Rael, Anthea
Ralph, Eileen
Ralph, Mrs. Francis
Rathbone, Joyce
Rawlins, Bessie
Rawlinson, Selma
Read, Christine
Regence, Ilse
Reiss-Smith, Thelma
Rendall, Honor
Reynell, Lenore
Reynolds, Edie
Richards, Irene
Richards, Kate
Riddick, Kathleen
Rihill, Maude
Rixon, Esther
Robbins, Tessa
Robinson, Anne
Robinson, Dora
Robinson, Serena
Robinson, Wendy
Robinson, Winifred
Robles, Marisa
Rogers, Meta
Rogers, Muriel
Rooke, Ethel
Rose, Diana
Rothwell, Evelyn
Rowe, Sally
Rozsa, Susanne
Rubinstein
Ruegg, Evelyn
Russell, Carol
Ryan, Jane
Ryan, Mary
Ryerson, Adna
Sadgrove, Pauline
Salmon, Jane
Sampson, Peggy
Sanders, F.G.
Saunders, Dorothy
Savory, Margaret
Sawyer, Mildred
Schein, Regina
Schlesinger, Winifred
Schulz, Erna
Scott, Marion
Scott, Pauline
Sellick, Phyllis
Semino, Norina
Serre, Daphne
Serruys
Seymour, Gertrude
Sharova, Alla
Sharpe, Rita
Shearer, Grace
Sheppard, Susan
Shinner, Emily
Shirley, Violet
Shuttleworth, Anna
Sichel, Brenda
Silver, Millicent
Simpson, Clare
Simons, Phyllis
Singleton, Joan
Sington, Louise
Sirnis, Gertrude
Slimmon
Slivko, Susan
Slocombe, Lizzie
Small, Gladys
Small, Winifred
Smith, Eleanor
Smith, Helen
Smith, Maureen
Smith, Winifred
Snow, Jessie
Snow, Ursula
Snowden, Marion
Solloway, Gloria
Solodchin, Galina
Sparrow, Sylvia
Speed, Clarisse
Spier, Irene
Spottiswoode, Daphne
Spurr, Phyllis
Squire, Julia
Stace, Lydia
Stamm, Ida
Stebbing, Margot
Steel, Gillian
Stell, Elsie
Stephens, Hilda
Stephenson, Ivy
Stewart, Jean
Stewart, Jessie
Stewart, Mary
St. George, Eleanor
Stiles, Winifred
Stirling, Dorothy
Stockbridge
Stockmarr, Johanne
Stone, Lucy
Stotesbury, Mercia
Street, Mrs. Edmund
Sturdy, Kathleen
Suart, Evelyn
Suppé, Anna von
Swain, Freda
Swale, Marguerite
Swann, Grace
Sweetland, Renee
Swepstone, Edith
Sworn, Inez
Talbot, May
Tate, Phillis
Taylor, Julie
Taylor, Muriel

Instrumentalists (contd.)

Taylor, Marilyn
Theobald, Minnie
Thomas, Frances
Thompson, Eveline
Thomas, Jeanne
Thompson, Jennifer
Thorburn
Thorndycraft, Rosemary
Thulliesm, Marie
Thurgood, Esther
Thynne, Grace
Timms, Eileen
Tookey, Elsa
Tookey, Muriel
Townshend, Jacqueline
Treseder, Dorothy
Trimby, Cecilia
Trotère
Trotter, Gwynneth
Troup, Josephine
Trowbridge, Valerie
Tunnell, Susan
Turnbull, Elizabeth
Vance, Edith
Vella, Mary
Verne, Adela
Verne, Mathilde
Verney, Olga
Vincent, Monica
Viscoma, Myra
Vogel, Edith
Wakeman, Daphne
Walenn, Dorothea
Walker, May
Wallace, Lucille
Wallis, Eunice
Ward, Theresa
Ward-Clarke, Jennifer
Warren, Eleanor
Watson, Joan
Weisberg, Zenie
Wells, Rosemary
Weston, Pamela
Whinyates, Seymour
White, Dora
White, Lesley
Whyte, Marjorie
Wieniawska, Elizabeth
Wild, Margaret
Williams, Anne
Williams, Mrs. Arthur
Williams, Gwendoline
Williams, Louise
Wills, Ann
Wilson, Brigid
Wilson, Marie
Wilson, Nora
Wilson, Shuna
Winter, Maud Agnes
Wise, Vera
Withers, Barbara
Withers, Mrs. Herbert
Wolfe, Anne
Wolfe, Nancy
Wood, Agnes
Wood, Dorothy
Wood, Lena
Woods, Beryl
Woods, Jacqueline
Woodward, Florence
Woodward, Phyllis
Woolley, Barbara
Wray, Elizabeth
Wright, Ada St. John
Wrigley, Yolande
Zorian, Olive

Messrs.

Ackeroyd, George
Acres, N.
Adamson, Michael
Adeney, Richard
Agate, E.
Alexander, Arthur
Alexander, Frederick
Alexandra, John
Alwyn William
Amherst, Nigel
Amory, A. Saint
Anderson, George
Anderson, Kinloch
Angel, David
Ansell, John
Appelbaum, Kurt
Armbruster, Carl
Aronowitz, Cecil
Aronowitz, John
Ashby, Arnold
Aspel, Simon
Attwell, Norman
Austin, Ernest
Austin, Frederic
Ayckbourn, Horace
Bailey, Mark
Bailey, Robert
Baillie, Alexander
Baines, Francis
Baker, Brian
Baker, Julian
Ball, Henry
Ball, Thalben
Ballardie, Quintin
Ballin, Arthur
Banham, William
Barbirolli, John
Barbour, Lyell
Baron, Gregory
Barritt, Paul
Bartlett, Alan
Barton, Gilbert
Barton, James
Barylli, Walter
Basseux, Pierre
Baster, Miles
Bateman, W.
Batty, Thomas
Bauer, Harold
Baumer, Cecil
Bean, Hugh
Beaven, John
Beaven, Peter
Beckwith, Arthur
Beel, Sigmund
Beers, Adrian
Beers, Ian

Instrumentalists (contd.)

Beeston, Michael
Behr, Edward
Belcher, Cecil
Bell, James
Benjamin, Arthur
Bennett, Gordon
Bennett, William
Bent, Arthur
Benthien, Ulrich
Bentley, Lionel
Berly, Harry
Bernard, Anthony
Best, Roger
Bilson, Robert
Binns, Malcolm
Birks, Ronald
Birnbaum, L.
Black, Neil
Blackburn, Robert
Blagrove, Stanley
Blakemore, Arthur
Blech, Harry
Bliss, Howard
Boase, Jack
Bochmann, Michael
Bohmer, L.
Bohr, Francis
Bonarius, Harold
Bonvalot, Cecil
Borlee, Victor
Borsdorf, Adolf
Borsdorf, Emil
Borsdorf, Francis
Borsdorf, Oskar
Borwick, A.
Borwick, Leonard
Bowen, L. Vincent
Bower, H.M.
Bowles, Horace
Bowman, Sidney
Boxall, Douglas
Bradley, Orton
Bradley, Hugh
Bradshaw, Martin
Brain, A.E.
Brain, Aubrey
Brain, A.E. jnr
Brain, Dennis
Brain, Leonard
Brainin, Norbert
Bratza
Bray, Eric
Brearly, John
Breethoff, W.C.
Bridger, Donald
Brightmore, W.
Brightwell, Edward
Bridge, Frank
Brinnen, Gerald
Bromley, Tom
Bronkhurst, Henry
Brooke, Gwydion
Brooke, Harold
Brookes, Dan
Brooks, Brian
Brosa, Antonio
Brown, Ian
Brown, Timothy
Brunet, Paul
Bryan, Gordon
Bryden, John
Brymer, Jack
Buchan, Gordon
Buchner, Willi
Buckoke, Peter
Buesst, Aylmer
Bunting, Christopher
Burden, John
Burrows, Vincent
Burrows, Vivian
Burton, Philip
Busby, T.R.
Busch, William
Bush, Alan
Buscher, Henri de
Butler, Mark
Butt, David
Butterworth, Oliver
Buxbaum, Friedrich
Bye, Charles
Caballero, Tapia
Cahn, Martin
Callow, Colin
Cameron, Douglas
Campbell, Arthur
Campbell, Colin
Carpenter, A.J.
Carter, Peter
Carter, W.B.
Carwardine, Edward
Cassini, Leonard
Cathie, Bewly
Cathie, George
Cathie, Philip
Caudle, Mark
Cave, Alfred
Cave, W.R.
Cazaubon, A.
Cernicoff, Vladimir
Chalk, Leonard
Chadwick, Brian
Chapman, G.P.
Chapman, Michael
Chapple, Norman
Chasey, Albert
Chauarri, Eduardo
Childe, Mantle
Christensen, E.A.
Chilingirian, Levon
Chilingworth, John
Christie, James
Civil, Alan
Clack, Peter
Clare, Maurice
Clark, James
Clark, Philip
Clark, Raymond
Clarke, Lionel
Clarke, Reginald
Clarke, William
Clarkson, Gustav
Clayton, Ivan
Clayton, Lennox
Clement, George
Clements, Alfred
Clifford, Julian

Instrumentalists (contd.)

Clinton, George
Cobbett, Walter
Cocks, P. Somers
Cohen, Raymond
Cohen, Robert
Coker, Paul
Cole, Peter
Cole, Maurice
Coleman, Joseph
Collingwood, J.A.
Collins, Anthony
Collett, Robert
Collingwood, L.A.
Comas, Nathan
Comberti, Sebastian
Connah, Geoffrey
Connah, Trevor
Cook, Leonard
Cooke, Charles R.
Cooke, Waddington
Coombs, George
Cooper, David
Cooper, Robert
Corbett, Geoffrey
Core, Henry I.
Corri, Vernon
Coull, Roger
Coulling, John
Courtraie, Leslie
Court, Andrew
Coverman, Charles
Cowen, Frederic
Cox, John
Crabbe, Charles
Cranmer, Arthur
Cranmer, Philip
Craxton, Harold
Crooke, Sidney
Cropper, Peter
Crowson, Lamar
Cruft, Benedict
Cruft, Eugene
Cruft, John
Cummings, Douglas
Cummings, Julian
Cummings, Keith
Cursue, Alfred
Curtis, David
Danks, Harry
Dalziell, Alan
Davies, E.W.
Davies, Ian
Davies, Ioan
Davies, John
Davies, Walford
Davis, Bernard
Davis, Howard
Davis, J.D.
Davison, Arthur
Davison, Munro
Dawson-Lyell, Julian
Decker, F.
Defauw, Désiré
Defosse, Henri
De Klijn, Nap
Del Mar, Norman
De Peyer, Gervase
De Ville, Claude
Dickinson, Hugh
Dight, Leonard
Doehaerd, Emile
Dolovitch, Max
Donovan, Stephen
Dorling, Cecil
Dossor, Lance
Dowding, Nicholas
Downes, Herbert
Doyle, A.K.
Draper, Charles
Draper, Charles jnr
Draper, H.P.
Draper, Paul
Dressel, Dettmar
Duprucq, Edward
Dugarde, Harry
Dulay, Arthur
Dunn, John
Dupré, Desmond
Dyer, John Y.
Dyke, Spencer
Easton, W.A.
Edwards, David
Edwards, Gwynne
Egerton, Julian
Egerton, Percy
Eisenberg, Maurice
Elias, John
Element, Ernest
Elinson, Iso
Elliot, Vernon
Ellis, Gregory
Ellis, Osian
Emms, Gerald
Enthoven
Epstein, Richard
Erdélyi, Csaba
Errington, Sidney
Essex, Kenneth
Evans, Archibald
Evans, Berian
Evans, Graham
Evans, Michael
Evans, Warwick
Evans, P.M.
Evans, Stephen
Fairhurst, Harold
Farjeon, Harry
Fawcett, Charlesworth
Fawcett, Verdi
Fell, Sidney
Fellowes, Horace
Ferber, Albert
Ferir, A.E.
Ferguson, Howard
Feuerman, John
Feuillard
Field, J.T.
Fincham, Sidney
Fisher, Cornelius
Flander, Bernard
Fleming, Victor
Fleury, Louis
Florac, John
Foggin, Myers
Fonteyne, J.L.

Instrumentalists (contd.)

Forbes, Watson
Ford, Allen
Foreman, Arthur
Forward, Charles
Foss, Hubert J.
Foster, Arnold
Foulds, J.H.
Francis, John
Frank, Alan
Frankel, Otto
Franklin, Norman
Fransella, Albert
Fransella, Henry
Fraser, John
Freudenthal, Otto
Freyhan, Michael
Friedman, Leonard
Friskin, James
Fry, William J.
Fryer, Herbert
Fudge, Roland
Gabarro, Francisco
Gallaway, Philip
Gallrein, Alfred
Gambold, Geoffrey
Gammie, Ian
García, José-Luís
Gardener, John
Garratt, Percival
Gasparini, Luigi
Gatt, Martin
Gaudo, Matzel
Gauntlett, Ambrose
Geiger, Hans
Gellhorn, Peter
George, Alan
Gibbs, James
Gibbs, Peter
Gibson, Henry
Gilbert, Max
Gilder, Tate
Gillard, Roy
Gillinson, Clive
Gilmer, Emile
Glasspool, W.
Glazier, Joshua
Glenton, Robert
Glickman, John
Goddard, Wilfred
Godwin, Paul
Golding, Miles
Goldstone, Anthony
Gomez, Manuel
Goodall, Reginald
Goodhead, C.
Goossens, Eugene
Goossens, Leon
Goren, Eli
Gottheiner, Max
Gough, Christopher
Gould, John
Gover, Gerald
Graeme, Peter
Graham, John
Grainger, Percy
Grande, Angel
Grant, Timothy
Grassi, Antonio de
Gravill, Alan
Gray, John
Gray, Stephen
Greaves, Ernest
Greenbaum, H.
Greenbaum, J.H.
Greenberg, Alfred
Greenslade, Hubert
Gregor-Smith, Bernard
Gregory, C.H.
Grey, F.C.
Griffith, Frederick
Griller, Sidney
Grimson, Robert
Grimson, Sam
Grimson, S. Dean
Grinke, Frederick
Gritton, Eric
Grondahl, Backer
Groote, Philip de
Groves, Vincent
Gruenberg, Alfons
Gruenberg, Erich
Grunebaum, Hermann
Günes, Rusen
Guy, Barry
Hacker, Alan
Halfpenny, E.E.
Hall, Edward Felix
Halling, Patrick
Halling, Peter
Hallis, Adolphe
Halsey, James
Hambleton, Hale
Hambourg, Charles
Hamburger, Paul
Hamilton, Iain
Hamlyn, Clifford
Hamlyn, Guy
Hampton, Colin
Hampton, Ian
Hancock, Maurice
Handy, Lionel
Hann, Clement
Hann, Lewis
Hann, William C.
Hann, W.H.
Hannah, Joseph
Hanson, Peter
Hardy, Lionel
Hare, Clayton
Harriot, Harold
Harris, Ronald
Harrison, Bertrand
Harrison, Eric
Harrison, Sidney
Hartley, Geoffrey
Hartung, F.
Harty, Hamilton
Harvey, Keith
Haslam, David
Hawkins, Brian
Hawkins, Frank
Hayward, L.B.
Head, Michael
Heath, Kenneth
Helden, Johann van

Instrumentalists (contd.)

Heley, John
Henkel, Karl
Hentschell, Wolfram
Hess, Jürgen
Heydrich
Hicks, H.C.S.
Hiller, Fritz
Hinchliff, Ernest
Hinchliff, W.
Hinds, Dennis
Hirsch, Leonard
Hobday, Alfred
Hobday, Claude
Hock, Johan C.
Hoffman, Israel
Holbrooke, Joseph
Holding, Frederic
Hollander, Jules
Holloway, John
Holmes, John
Holmes, Ralph
Holst, Henry
Hope, Eric
Hopkinson, Albert
Hopkinson, Ernest
Horgan, Brian
Horsley, Colin
Howard, Frank
Howard, William
Howells, Herbert
Hudson, Eli
Humphrey, Graeme
Humphreys, Sydney
Humphries, Ian
Hundt, Hugo
Hunerfurst, Hugo
Hunt, John
Hurlstone, William Y.
Hurwitz, Emanuel
Hurwitz, Michael
Hutchinson, George
Hyde, Alan
Hyde-Smith, Christopher
Igloi, Thomas
Imhof, Charles
Ineson, Ernest
Iorio, Luciano
Ireland, John
Ireland, Patrick
Ireland, Robin
Isaacs, Edward
Isaacs, George
Isaacs, Harry
Isaacs, Kelly
Isepp, Martin
Isserlis, Steven
Jackson, Frederick
Jackson, Garfield
Jacobs, Archie
Jacobson, Maurice
Jackson, Frederic
James, Cecil
James, E.F.
James, Ifor
James, Ivor
James, Wilfred
Janser, Georg
Jenkins, Rae
Jeremy, Raymond
Jewel, Ian
Joachim, Robert
Jones, Darbishire
Jones, Granville
Jones, Michael
Jones, Norman
Jones, Stuart
Jones, Trevor
Jongen, Joseph
Jonson, Guy
Joseph, Vivian
Joubert, Jules
Kahn, Percy B.
Kampen van, C.
Kanga, Homi
Kastner, Alfred
Katin, Peter
Katz, Paul
Kay, Richard C.
Kaznowski, Michal
Keenlyside, Raymond
Keith, Charlton
Keith, Pusey
Kell, Reginald
Kellett, Colin
Kelly, Daniel
Kelly, S. Kneale
Kennard, Benjamin
Kentleton, A.G.
Kerrison, William
Kessler, Jack
Kiddle, F.B.
King, Russell
Kinsey, Herbert
Kinsey, W.R.
Kirsch, Sigmund
Kitcat, J.L.
Knight, Edgar
Knight, John
Knott, Handel
Knussen, Stuart
Koeckert, Rudolf
Kok, Alexander
Kok, Felix
Krall, Emil
Krause, Henry
Kreuz, Emil
Krish, Serge
Kummer, F.
Kutcher, Samuel
Laffitte, Frank
Lagrilliere, M.
Lait, Harkness
Lake, Ian
Lalande, Désiré
Lale, Peter
Lamb, Anthony
Lamport, Brian
Landa, Albert
Lander, Clive
Lang, Andrew
Langrish, Vivian
Laoureux, Marcel
Latchem, Malcolm
Laulund, Jorgen
Lawrence, E.C.

Instrumentalists (contd.)

Ledger, Philip
Ledig, Martin
Leeuwen Boomkamp, Carel van
Leighton-Brown, Howard
Leipold, George
Leipold, J.B.
Lemmone, John
Leppard, Sydney
Leonard, Lawrence
Leslie, W.H.
Lester, Harold
Lester, Richard
Levesley, Neil
Levey, B.
Levey, Henry
Levey, James
Levine, Adrian
Levy, Philip
Lewcowitsch, Lason
Lewis, Anthony
Liddle, Samuel
Liebe, Theodor
Livsey, R.
Loban, Maurice
Lockyer, James
Loewenguth, Alfred
Logie, Nicholas
Lord, Roger
Loveday, Alan
Loveday, Martin
Lovelock, J.F.
Lovell, Keith
Lovett, Martin
Lovey, Alfred
Lovey, Alphonse
Ludwig, Paul
Lumby, H.
Lynch, Charles
Lythgoe, Clive
McCabe, John
McCaw, John
McCarthy, John
McConnell, F.
Macdonald, George
McGavin, Andrew
McGee, Robin
McGegan, Nicholas
MacIntyre, Ian
Macon
Macmahon, Ivor
Maddren, Harold
Magrath, Guy
Maguire, Hugh
Malcolm, George
Malsch, W.M.
Mangeot, André
Mann, Adolph
Mann, T.E.
Mannheimer, Frank
Mannucci, Livio
Manoliu, Petru
Manser, John
Manton, Victor
Manuel, William
Margetson, E.J.
Marinari, Gaston
Markbreiter, Felix
Markham, Peter
Marriner, Andrew
Marriner, Neville
Marson, John
Martin, Christopher
Martin, David
Martin, Thomas
Marwood, Christopher
Mason, Berkeley
Mason, Carlton
Mason, Edward
Mason, J.
Mason, Timothy
Masters, Robert
Matthews, David
Matthews, Denis
Mayer, Maurice
Maynard, Bryan
Melsa
Merrick, Frank
Merrett, J. Edward
Merrett, James W.
Merz, Josef
Mews, Walter
Mierowski
Miles, Percy H.
Milne, Hamish
Moeran, E.J.
Mohr, G.A.
Moiseiwitsch, Benno
Money, David
Mont, Willem de
Montandon, J.J.
Moore, Gerald
Moore, John
Morel
Morgan, R. Orlando
Morley, Reginald
Morressy, W.F.
Morris, G. O'Connor
Morris, Gareth
Morris, Henry
Morris, Tom F.
Morrison, Angus
Morrison, T.H.
Moser, Fritz
Mozin, Leon
Muller, Georg
Muller, Rudolf Maria
Mulliner, Michael
Muncey, Richard
Mundy, John
Murby, T.
Murgier, Jacques
Murphy, George
Murray, Nigel
Muskett, B.J.
Nash, Stewart
Neaman, Yfrah
Nemes, Desider
Newhouse, A.
Newton, H.A.
Newton, Ivor
Newton, Richard
Nissel, Sigmund
Nitland, Pieter

Instrumentalists (contd.)

Norris, Robert
Norton, Arthur
Nunn, Richard
Nunn, Walter
O'Brien, Edward
O'Brien, Jack
O'Donnell, Manus
Ogden, David
Olive, John
O'Neal, Christopher
O'Neill, Norman
D'Oliveira, Louis
O'Reilly, Brendan
Orton, Stephen
Osborn, Franz
Otscharkoff, Theodor
Ould, Charles
Ould, Percy
Outram, Martin
Ovens, Raymond
Padel, William
Page, Martin
Palmer, George
Parker, B. Patterson
Parker, Nicholas
Parker-Smith, Geoffrey
Parkhouse, David
Parikian, Manoug
Parkin, Eric
Parry, Wilfrid
Parsons, Geoffrey
Parsons, Herbert
Parsons, H.O.
Pascal, Julian
Patterson, Austin
Patterson, Martyn
Pauer, John
Paul, Reginald
Payne, John
Peachey, Frederick
Pearce, F.S.
Pearson, Ian
Pearson, Justin
Peatfield, Thomas
Pecker, Boris
Peel, Graham
Pennington, John
Perfect, Dudley
Peros, Henri
Perry, Arnold
Peruzzi
Pessak, Joseph
Pettinger, Peter
Pettit, David
Pettit, William H.
Petre, Thomas R.
Philippe, Geoffrey
Phillipowsky, Ivan
Phillips, Charles
Phillips, Harvey
Phillips, Herbert
Phillips, John
Physick, Tom
Pigneguy, John
Pinfield, Gilbert
Pini, Anthony
Pini, Carl
Pinto, David
Pirani, Max
Pleeth, William
Plimmer, H.G.
Plowitz, Théodor
Podusgka, Wolfgang
Pointer, John
Pollard, Claude
Pollitzer, A.
Polonaski, E.
Pook, Jack
Poole, H.J.
Pople, Peter
Pople, Ross
Popperwell, Stanley
Potts, Hugh
Pougnet, Jean
Powell, Lloyd
Power, John Story
Prade, Ernest La
Pratley, Geoffrey
Pratt, Ross
Preedy, Cyril
Preuveneers, C.
Preuveneers, J.
Preuxt, Cornelis
Prévost, Germain
Price, Walter
Primrose, William
Probyn, Frank
Proctor, Charles
Puddy, Keith
Purrier, Vincent J.
Puttick, A.J.
Quaife, Edwin W.
Quilter, Roger
Ralph, Horace
Randall, Anthony
Raphael, Roger
Rawlinson, Harold
Read, Frank
Read, W.J.
Reed, W.H.
Reeves, George
Reeves, H. Wynn
Reillie, Bernard
Reisacher, Louis
Reizenstein, Franz
Renard, Jacques
Renesse, George
Rennell, E.
Reuland, Leon
Reynolds, Bernard
Reynolds, Frank
Reynolds, John
Reynolds, Thomas
Reynolds, Wynford
Rice, Eric
Richards, Bernard
Richardson, Alan
Richardson, W.
Rickelman, Boris
Riddell, Duncan
Riddle, Frederick
Riedl, Oscar F.
Rignold, Hugo
Ring, Layton
Roberts, Bernard

Instrumentalists (contd.)

Robertson, Paul
Robertson, Rae
Robinson, Bernard
Robinson, Edward J.
Robinson, Eric
Robinson, Martin
Robson, Paul
Roche, Roger
Roese, L.
Roever, J.
Röntgen, Joachim
Rooke, John
Rooke, Philip A.
Rosenheim, Samuel
Rosenstein, Meyer
Rosenthal, Julian
Rostall, Julius
Roth, David
Roth, George
Rouse, Stephen
Routledge, Ernest
Rowland, Christopher
Rowland-Jones, Simon
Rubbra, Edmund
Rubens, Leonard
Rubinstein, Leonard
Russell, Sheridan
Sainton, Phillip
Salkeld, F.
Salmond, Felix
Salpeter, Max
Sammons, Albert
Sampson, Bryan
Samuel, Harold
Sandeman, David
Sandby, Herman
Sanders, Mark
Sanders, Neill
Sandford, Arthur
Saram, Druvi de
Saram, Rohan de
Saunders, John
Sauer, Colin
Schatzberger, Leslie
Schidlof, Peter
Schiele, Brian
Schiller, Allan
Schilsky, Charles
Schmidt, Gustav
Schmitt, Florent
Schonberger, Benno
Schrattenholz
Schrecker, Bruno
Schroder, Jaap
Schulman, Andrew
Schwiller, Isidore
Schwiller, Jean
Scott, Ernest
Scott, Gilderoy
Scott, Graeme
Scott, Willy
Sealey, John
Seiber, Matyas
Sermon, Peter
Shadwick, Joseph
Sharp, Ian
Sharpe, Cedric
Sharpe, Herbert
Shea, S.V.
Shedlock, J.S.
Sherrin, James
Shillito, Martin
Shinebourne, Jack
Shingles, Stephen
Shore, Bernard
Shorter, A.J.
Sillito, Kenneth
Silverman, Edward
Silverthorne, Paul
Silvester, Jack
Simmons, G.
Simms, Philip
Simonetti, Achile
Simons, Dennis
Simons, John
Simpson, Derek
Simpson, Robert Hope
Sisserman, David
Skeaping, Kenneth
Skeaping, Roderick
Slater, Joseph
Slocombe, A.J.
Smerdon, J.L.
Smith, Alexander
Smith, Cyril
Smith, David
Smith, Roger
Snowden, John
Sobrino, Carlos
Solomon
Solomon, Yonty
Somervell, Arthur
Sons, Maurice
Southward, C.
Southwell, William
Southworth, W.P.
Soutter, James
Sparey, Jonathan
Speight, Joseph
Spinks, Charles
Spivak, Eli
Srawley, Stephen
St. Amory, A.
Stanbridge, Roland
Standage, Simon
Stanford, Charles V.
Stanley, Norris
Stanley, Peter
Staryk, Steven
Staveley, Colin
Stehling
Stein, Leonard
Stephens, Rex
Stevens, Derek
Stevens, Peter
Stevens, William
Stever, Manuel
Stone, David
Stone, Frederick
Straeten, van der
Stratton, George
Street, Oscar W.
Street, R.
Streets, John
Strub, Harald

Instrumentalists (contd.)

Stryckers, Piet
Stubbs, Harry
Stutfield, G.L.
Such, Henry
Such, Percy
Sutch, W.
Sutcliffe, J.
Sutcliffe, Sidney
Sutcliffe, Wallace
Sutherland, Robert
Sutton, Graham
Sutton, W.
Szabo, Paul
Szczepanowski, L.
Tabb, R.V.
Talagrand, Paul
Talbot, J.E.
Tapia-Caballero
Tapping, Roger
Tattersdill, John
Taylor, Carl
Taylor, Coleridge
Taylor, David
Taylor, Handel
Tchaikowsky, André
Tees, Stephen
Tertis, Lionel
Thomas, Geoffrey
Thomas, Martin
Thomas, Peter
Thomas, Ronald
Thomson, Bothwell
Thomson, Douglas
Thorndycraft, Ronald
Thurston, Frederick
Ticciati, Francesco
Ticehurst, John
Tidmarsh, Egerton
Tildesley, Richard
Tinney, Hugh
Tomlinson, Ernest
Treiber, C.
Trethowen, William
Trew, Arthur
Triggs, H.T.
Trussler, John
Trust, H.T.
Tucker, Norman
Tuckwell, Barry
Tunnell, Charles
Tunnell, John
Turner, Cecil
Turner, Harold
Turner, Lawrence
Turnland, George
Turton, Peter
Twelvetrees, Clive
Underwood, Bryan
Underwood, John
Vallier, John
Vandermeerschen, H.
Van Heuvel, John
Vegh, Sandor
Verity, James
Victor, Charles
Vigay, Denis
Virgo, Edwin
Visman, Daniel
Vleet, Herbert van
Wakefield, Jeffrey
Walding, F.
Walenn, Arthur
Walenn, Gerald
Walenn, Herbert
Walker, Edward
Walker, Ernest
Walker, Gordon
Waller, Ronald
Wallfisch, Peter
Wallfisch, Raphael
Wallis, William
Walthew, Richard H.
Walthew, R.S.
Walton, John
Wang, Alfredo
Ward, Max
Ward, Paul
Ward, William
Warner, H. Waldo
Warnock, Felix
Waterhouse, William
Waterman, David
Waters, Stephen
Watson, Victor
Waud, J. Haydn
Waud, J.P.
Waud, S.P.
Waud, W.V.
Webbe, Herbert
Weber, Carl
Webster, H. Smith
Weil, Terence
Weiner
Weingarten, Joseph
Weist-Hill, Ferdinand
Weist-Hill, T.E.
Weitz-Guy
Wellington, Christopher
Wellingham, John
Welsh, Moray
Werge, Tennyson
Wertheim, S.L.
Wessely, Hans
West, Harold
Wetherell, Eric
Wethmar, Nobert
Wheeler, Nigel
Whitaker, George
White, Ian
White, John
Whitehead, James
Whitehouse, W.E.
Whitfield, Ernest
Whiting, Nicolas
Whitsey, Fred
Whittaker, Douglas
Wightman, Tom
Wilde, Barry
Wildman, H.
Willaume
Williams, Andrew
Williams, Arthur
Williams, A.B.
Williams, C
Williams, F.
Williams, Gerrard

Instrumentalists (contd.)

Williams, H.
Williams, Jeremy
Williams, Jonathan
Williams, Trevor
Willison, Peter
Willoughby, Louis
Wills, John
Wilson, Edward
Wilson, Rolf
Wiltshire, Walter
Winkler, Wilhelm
Winterbottom, Charles
Wise, David
Withers, Herbert
Wolstenholme, W.
Wood, D.S.
Wood, F.
Wood, Haydn
Wood, Henry J.
Wood, M.
Wood, Robin
Woolhouse, Edmund
Wotton, T.
Wotton, W.
Yates, George
Yonge, Ernest
Yosilevsky, Maurice
Yovanovitch, Dushko
Ysaÿe, Theo
Zacharewitsch, Michael
Zerbini, J.B.
Zimmermann, Louis
Zoldy, Sandor

VOCALISTS

Mesdames

A'Bear, Magdalena
Allen, Mrs. Perceval
Amit, Sheila
Anderson, Victoria
Andrews, Alice A.
Andvjar, Carmen
Appleton, Ruby
Arden, Evelyn
Arnell, Dora
Baker, Janet
Balfour, Margaret
Bannerman, Betty
Barnard, Dora
Barter, Margaret
Barth, Alice
Bartlett, Edith
Beaufort, Beatrice
Beazley, Mabel
Beck, Ellen
Beetlestone, Ethel
Bennett, Dorothy
Berger, Lillian
Bevans, Ethel
Biddell, Cassie
Billington, D.
Bissett, Margaret
Blain, Helen
Blinkhorn, Marian
Blyth, May
Bonnin, Mary
Borodine, Alma
Bott, Paula
Boxius, Rosa
Braine, Mabel
Brandt, Katherine
Brani, Cecile
Braun, Irma
Brama, Marie
Bramner, Florence
Briggs, Emily
Brony, Otta
Brooks, Phyllis
Buck, Jean
Burch, C.N.
Busby, May
Cable, Margaret
Cardozo, Cecilia
Carlton, Eveleen
Carter, Gwendoline
Cathie, Mrs. Philip
Catley, Gwen
Cattaned, Eva
Chatterton, Vivienne
Cherry, Kate
Christie, Florence
Christopher, Janet
Clapp, Ethel
Clapp, Mabel
Clark, Dorothy
Clegg, Edith
Cody, Kathleen
Coleman, Esther
Collier, Louise
Collins, Flora
Colton, Nora
Cooper, Ida
Corran, Mabel
Cosslett, Gwen
Cramer, Pauline
Creser
Compton, Dorothea
Cropper, Sybil
Cross, Joan
Crowley, Iseult
Damian, Grace
Davidson, Emma
Davies, Maggie
Davies, S.
Dawney, Nora
Defosse, Elizabeth
D'Espagne, Jeanne
Dewhurst, Amy
Dorow, Dorothy
D'Orsay, Dorothy
Douglas, Kate
Downes, Evelyn
Dresser, Marcia van
Dreux, Edmée de
Elliott, Maude
Elton, J.
Elwes, Joan
Fassett, Isabel
Feltesse

Vocalists (contd.)

Fenton, Ethel
Ffrangcon-Davies, Gwen
Fischer, Sarah
Florac
Florence, Evangeline
Foster, Megan
Foster, Muriel
Fowler, M.
Fraser, Janet
Gale, Ursula
Gandy, Dorothy
Gardner, Lilian
Gaskell
Gerard, Louise
Gillett, Ettie
Goodwin, Lucy
Gough, Beatrice
Graham, Thelma
Grant, Kathleen
Gray, Lissa
Grey, Mary
Griffith, Mrs. Yeatman
Gruhn, Nora
Gutteres, A. Maude
Hamilton-Smith, Janet
Hamlin, Mary
Hann, Marianne
Harford, Vida
Harland
Harris, R.
Harrison, Marjorie
Hatfield, Frances
Heale, Alice
Hearne, Isabel
Heath, Muriel
Heddeghem, Blanche van
Helmrich, Dorothea
Henden-Warde
Henschel, Helen
Hensler, Edith
Heyermans, Felicie
Hickson, W.
Holbrook, Kate
Howison, Margaret
Hughes, Helena
Hughes, Muriel
Humphrys, Bertini
Hutchinson
Ide, Carlotta
Inglis, Gertrude
Jackson, Hope
Janes, E.
Jennings, Betty
Joachim, Gabriele
Johnstone, Kate
Joliet, Marie
Jones, Dilys
Jones, Hanna
Jouve, Jeanne
Kertinge, Merwyn
Kennedy-Fraser
Kerr, Grainger
Kiddier, Ida
Kimber, Evelyn
King, Jessie
Kirkwood, Edith
Kitchen, Dorothy
Knightly, Amy
Kreuz, Fannie
Labbette, Dora
Lake, Mollie
Larkcom, Agnes
Lawson, Winifred
Layton, Annie
Leighton, Clara
Lenoir, Lucie
Leo, Rosa
Licette, Miriam
Lido, Marie de
Liess, Lotte
Lindsay, Mary
Loaring, Ada
Londa, Alice
Lowe, Anne
Lund, Mary
Lyon, Elisabeth
Macaulay, Gertrude
Mackerras, Margarita
Macnally, Mary
McBride, Annie
McClure, Christine
McCreith, Christine
McCullagh, Edith
McKenzie, Marian
Maden, Sybil
Maitland, Lena
Makower, M.
Makushina, Tatiana
Mandeville, Alice
Mann, Flora
Mansfield, Veronica
Marchesi, Blanche
Marion, Ruth
Marmion, Alanna
Marshall, Eleanor
Martin, Alice
Marwood, Winifred
Maryska, Nan
Mason, Delia
Mattingley, May
Mawhinney, E.
May, Elsa
Middleton, Muriel
Mills, Daisy
Minns, Marilyn
Moger, Gladys
Moir, A.
Monk, M.
Montagu-Conyers
Monteith, Zippora
Moore, Margaret
Morgan, Eugenia
Morgan, Molly de
Morley, Annie
Morris, Olive
Morris, Viola
Morse, Rose
Morton, Nonie
Moulton, Dorothy
Muirella, Joan
Mullen, Adelaide
Murray, Stella
Neale, Eva
Neovi, Saima
Nettleship, Ursula
Nevine, Nin

Vocalists (contd.)

Newton, Joyce
Nicolls, Agnes
Nielsen, Flora
Nixon, Muriel
Oakeshott, Alice
Oliver, Florence
O'Neill, Myra
Ormsby, Louise
Osborne, Eleanore
Osborne, Thelwyn
Page, Lilian
Parkin, Valerie
Parry, Elian
Patterson, Ada
Paul, Cedar
Percival, Edith
Perregaux, Alexia
Philips, Ivy
Phillips, Louise
Pironnay, Fernande
Pironnay, Mary
Pisani, Elvira
Plowitz, Paula
Polanski, Thérèse
Purves, Allison
Purvis, Maggie
Pye, J.
Quentin, Erna
Quick, Selina
Raine, Jeannette
Ralph, Eileen
Rea, Marianne
Rickaby, Phyllis
Ritchie, Margaret
Robinson, Ethel
Robinson, Rina
Robson, Clara
Robson, Dorothy
Rollet, Marguerite
Roosevelt, Hilda
Rosen, Carole
Russell, Violet
St. André
St. Claire, Meriel
Sales, N.
Salter, Bertha
Salter, Florence
Saunders, Marguerite
Scanes, Sybil
Scott, Gilderoy
Scott, Monica
Scott, Phyllis
Seabrooke, Elliott
Seager, N.E.
Shaw, Florence
Shuard, Amy
Simon, Eleanor Cleaver
Simpson, Hebe
Smith, Janet Dunlop
Smith, O. Etherington
Sobrino
Sole, Sara
Sonnenberg, Jenny
Spencer, Beatrice
Stamm, Lorna
Stevens, Dora
Stuckey, Isabel
Stevenson, Evelyn
Stewart, Catherine
Susman, Sara
Swinton, Elsie
Taggart, Jenny
Thornfield, Emily
Thursfield, Anne
Thynne, Belle
Tomlinson, Mary
Trenton, Louise
Trollope, Dorothy
Truscott, Euneta
Trust, Helen
Turner, Frances
Turner, Norah Scott
Turner, Palgrave
Turrell, Celia
Urbankova, Tonci
Venning, Alice
Verney, Myra
Walker, Mrs. Hyde
Ward, Millicent
Waterson, Jean
Watson, Mildred
Webb, Dorothea
Weber-Delacre, Marie Ann
Wild, Margaret
Williams, Nora O.
Wilson, Hilda
Witting, Agnes
Wolf, Ilse
Wood, Mrs. Henry J.
Wormald, Lillie
Wyss, Colette
Wyss, Sophie
Zachner, Lilly

Messrs.

Abor, Wilfrid
Acfield, Wilfrid
Ackroyd, Roderick
Adams, John
Alexander, Arthur
Alexander, Harry
Allen, Gerald
Andrews, John J.
Austin, Frederic
Austin, Sumner
Ayres, D. Byndon
Ayrton, Bertram
Bailey, Gilbert
Bailey, Haydn G.
Bannister, Maurice
Barker, Frank
Beaumont, Henry
Bell, Mostyn
Bertram, Ernest
Birch, Ernest
Bonner, Arthur
Booth, A.E.
Booth, John
Borwell, Montague
Bovett, James A.
Bowen, Kenneth
Bowers, Sydney
Brand, James
Braun, Francis
Brereton, W.H.
Bromilow, Hubert

Vocalists (contd.)

Brooks, Ernest
Broomfield, A.W.
Brown, Vernon
Brown, W.
Brynley, David
Buckley, John
Callan, J.H.
Carne, Victor
Carnegie, Austen
Carey, Clive
Chignell, Robert
Child, Harry
Cleather, Gordon
Clive, Franklin
Coates, John
Coffin, Hayden
Colyer, Owen
Connell, Horatio
Connery, Frank
Cooper, Hayes
Copland, Charles
Corner, Henry J.
Coryn, A.
Cranmer, Arthur
Cruz, Juan de la
Cummings, Henry
Cunliffe, Wilfrid
Dance, Thomas
Davey, Murray
Davidson, Reginald
Davies, Madoc
Davies, Morgan
Davis, Osmond
De Peyer, Everard
Dickie, Murray
Dixon, A. Capel
Dossor, Seymour
Dunn, Geoffrey
Eisdell, Hubert
Elwes, Gervase
Evans, Sackville
Faithful, Rex
Falkner, Keith
Ferguson, A. Foxton
Fleet, Edgar
Flegg, Bruce
Ford, Walter
Forington, William
Freer, Dawson
Fry, Howard
Fuller, Frederick
Galliver, David
Gatfield, Edward
Gibbs, Cynlais
Gleeson, Frank
Godfrey, Louis
Goodey, Tom
Goss, John
Gould, Gordon
Greene, Eric
Greene, H. Plunket
Grice, Robert
Griffith, Yeatman
Groom, Ernest
Gye, E. Fanning
Habbijam, Frederic
Halford, John
Hamilton, William
Hammond-Stroud, D.
Hanneson, Thornsteinn
Harding, Victor
Harford, Francis
Hast, Gregory
Hastwell, Frank C.
Head, Michael
Henderson, Roy
Henry, Julien
Henschel, George
Higley, William
Hodgson, George W.
Holland, R.
Holmes, Laurence
Holmes, Leslie
Honey, Gordon
Hosking, Frederic
Hunter, Riddell
Irwin, Robert
Jay, Eustace
Jones, Hirwen
Jones, Parry
Jordan, Arthur
Joubert, E.
Joynt, Scott
Keel, Frederick
Kelsey, Franklyn
Keyte, Christopher
Klitgaard, Manitto
Kyle, Richard
Lane, Bernard
Laughton, Sidney
Laurie, Vere
Lavary, Jacques
Layton, Alfred J.
Lensky, Boris
Ley, James H.
Lierhammer, Theo
Lilley, Norman
Linley, G.R.
Loder, Ernest
Logan, Sinclair
Loring, Francis
Lowther, Brabazon
Luxon, Benjamin
McCormack, John
McInnes, J. Campbell
McKenna, John
Mace, W.
Maitland, Robert
Manchester, Percy
Marion, Sidney
Marshall, Eric
Marsland, Septimus
Matters, Arnold
Maxwell, William R.
Metcalfe, Eric
Mirsky, M.
Milner, Augustus
Mitton, Whitworth
Montefiore, Eade
Morel, John
Morgan, Ben
Mostyn, Courtnay
Murphy, Jerome
Nadejin, Nikolai
Noble, Dennis
Norman, C.

Vocalists (contd.)

Northcote, Sydney
Notley, Norman
O'Mara, Joseph
O'Sullivan, Denis
Parker, George
Parsons, Basil
Partridge, Ian
Patzak, Julius
Paull, William
Pearson, G. Cullen
Peyton, Hugh
Phillips, Frank
Pizzey, George
Powell, Claud
Probert, John
Ranalow, Frederick
Raphael, Mark
Ray, Charles
Reed, George Wilber
Reilly, Ereach
Ross, B.
Rosslyn, Howell
Rulf, P.R.
Sapsed, Charles
Saunders, Charles
Shirley-Quirk, John
Schock, Rudolf
Simmonds, Herbert
Simon, Ingo
Smith, Cuthbert
Smith, Dale
Snowden, Percy
Soames, René
Spark, S.H.
Spicer, Earle
Standage, Silas
Stone, Norman
Streatfield, Richard
Strickland, R.E.
Stroesco, Constantin
Taylor, Arthur
Thomson, Marcus
Thorndike, Herbert
Till, Charles
Tinayre, Yues
Tomes, Phillips
Topping, James
Tudor, Kenneth
Turnpenny, Henry
Varian, William
Victor, Charles
Walenn, Arthur
Wharton, Edward
Wendon, Henry
White, Walter
Wilde, Harold
Wilhelmj, August
Wilson, Chilver
Wilson, H. Lane
Wilson, Stewart
Woodhouse, Frederick
Yates, Reginald
Young, Alexander

THE CONCERT COMMITTEE (1887-1987)

The Misses
K. Abrahams (2)
V.A. Alexander (5)
A. Andrews (3)
Arklay (6)
Arnfield (1)
F. Arnold (6)
Barbere (4)
B. Barralet (4)
Barry (2)
F. Becham (8)
A. Bentley (7)
M. Bumpus (2)
L. Burke (7)
R. Bush (2)
Camerman (3)
A. Carpenter (20)
G. Catherall (4)
H. Catherall (20)
B. Channing (8)
D. Chappell (4)
I. Clappé (6)
H. Crutchlow (see Mrs. Minchin)
J. Crutchlow (4)
S. Crutchlow (1)
G. Davison (3)
M.G. Downs (1)
S. Eakins (4)
I. Evans (8)
* H.M. Fairhall (20)
P. Fenton (2)
George (1)
Gibson (1)
E.F. Gillard (2)
H.R. Godfrey (2)
A. Gould (9)
G. Gowing (3)
R. Halls (42)
L.C. Harris (2)
V. Hassid (18)
Henman (1)
Hochfeld (3)
M. Howard (2)
A.M. Howship (7)
L. Isaacs (1)
E. Ivimey (8)
K. Jarrett (8)
M. Keatinge (2)
H. Langelaan (11)
L. Levison (1)
G.T. Lewis (1)
F. Lidstone (2)
H. Lidstone (6)
R. Lister (1)
F.E. Marquardt (3)
W.J. Meadmore (2)
A. Monro (2)
M. O'Brien (1)
E. Palmer (2)
N. Parker (1)
Partington (4)
M. Pitts (3)
A. Pugh (3)
E. Pugh (2)
I. Reynolds (1)
R. Rosenberg (2)
J. Rowley (see Mrs. Hutchinson)
L.A. Salmon (2)
R. Salmon (3)
M. Seeley (see Mrs. Lincé)
E. Shorter (2)
L.M. Simes (6)
A. Simmons (1)
A.E. Simons (7)
E. Simons (18)
F.J. Simons (40)
M. Skellhorn (1)
J. Smith (2)
P. Snelling (52)
S. Sowter (19)
E. Stich (3)
V. Stuttig (3)
M. Sumner (2)
E. Swepstone (5)
M. Taylor (2)
S. Toms (2)
C. Tresidder (2)
L. Usherwood (3)
M.J. Ville (1)
F.M. Ville (see Mrs. Hawkins)
A. Weston (1)
Wilcox (2)
W. Williams (1)

Mesdames
A. Andrews (3)
Y. Awbery (3)
E. Barralet (12)
F. Barralet (1)
K. Barralet (1)
Blackburn (7)
M. Blake (2)
E.W. Blakemore (4)
I.M. Briscoe (13)
H. Brown (20)
G. Bunn (2)
I. Burall (12)
* D.M. Clements (27)
J. Costello (2)
L.T. Davies (4)
C.M. Dowse (4)
M. Elton (1)
C. Fletcher-Smith (6)
D.M. Galin (5)
I. Goldesgeyme (4)
C. Goodwin (1)
* F.M. Hawkins (42)
E. Hicks (20)
H. Hooper (7)
C.K. Hutcheon (1)
* J. Hutchinson (43)
M. Idiens (4)
E. Lacey (2)
M. Lincé (43)
D. Lindsay (4)
T.C. Lindsay (4)
S. Meadmore (3)
H. Minchin (18)

C.K. Osborne (13)
E.G. Overy (2)
D. Paine (5)
M. Roth (17)
J. Sainsbury (7)
K. Seeley (10)
D.M. Simmons (3)
Stanbury (1)
R. Warwick (4)
A. Watson (12)
Westaway (1)

Messrs

J. Aldred (3)
* A.E. Anderson (1)
* A. Andrews (15)
G. Andrews (2)
R. Ardley (1)
E.H. Atkinson (5)
J. Badcock (2)
W.F. Barnett (2)
C. Barralet (33)
E. Barralet (2)
S. Barralet (4)
H. Bastow (1)
H.J. Beard (1)
A.G. Bell (1)
E.G. Biaggini (2)
J. Birnbaum (9)
H. Blake (5)
E.K. Blyth (1)
C.R. Brace (1)
J. Brebner (5)
S. Brissenden (5)
C. Browne (14)
G. Bunn (7)
L. Camerman (17)
F.W. Canning (31)
C. Carwardine (4)
C.A. Carwardine (4)
E. Carwardine (2)
R. Cassidy (3)
G. Catherall (8)
*A.J. Clements (51)
F. Constable (5)
P. Costello (12)
F. Cresswell (20)
W. Crowder (2)
E. Cunningham (26)
W. Deadman (1)
H.W. Dixon (1)
P. Dixon (1)
G.C. Dowman (1)
P. Dowman (1)
G.M. Dowse (1)
G. Elkan (3)
J. Elkan (2)
* L. Elton (3)
*G.W. Evans (3)
R.H. Evans (10)
C. Fairhall (4)
E.J. Fairhall (2)
*T. Fairhall (3)
G.H. Fenn (3)
A.E. Fenton (7)
C. Fenton (1)
W.H. Fenton (6)
I. Finkel (3)
W. Fish (8)
J. Fraser (2)
F. Gent (3)
F. Freeman (1)
M. Goldesgeyme (21)
H. Gould (3)
H.B. Gowing (3)
J.L. Green (4)
W. Greenberg (1)
W. Halliday (6)
C. Hanselmann (2)
L.C. Harrison (2)
F.G. Hasthorpe (2)
*F.A. Hawkins (43)
* F.V. Hawkins (42)
P.A. Hawkins (1)
E.H. Hennig (1)
H.C.S. Hicks (3)
G. Hickson (3)
D. Hinds (1)
O. Hooper (10)
W. Horsley (2)
H. Hunns (8)
J.A. Hutcheon (3)
*G. Hutchinson (55)
F. James (2)
A. Jermy (11)
B.J. Kensit (7)
E.S. King (3)
G. Kuttner (3)
T.R. Lawson (1)
E. Liers (3)
*A.M. Lincé (40)
L. Lindsay (11)
M. Lines (1)
*C.E. Lister (10)
W. Maidstone (28)
E.H. Maier (2)
Mandel (1)
T.S. Mansford (6)
W. Mansford (10)
A. May (1)
W.A. Meadmore (3)
*W.S. Meadmore (3)
J. Metcalf (3)
*W. Morressy (3)
*H.G. Morris (16)
F.W. Munns (3)
H. Myers (1)
V.L. Nash (2)
F.M. Overy (1)
H. Parry (6)
J. Pezaro (2)
A.N. Pocock (1)
A.E. Rackley (1)
F.A. Reichert (1)
A. Reiss (15)
W.T. Restadd (6)
J.W. Roberts (2)
L. Roth (17)
H.H. Rothery (1)
F. St. Aubin (11)
G.N. Salmon (8)
H. Schick (4)
E.P. Service (7)
*F. Service (8)
H. Seyler (8)
F. Shaw (2)
H.T. Shaw (1)